Flavours of Istanbul

A Selection from Original 19th

Century Ottoman Recipes

medya+ik

medya+ik 2007/15
Cookbook/06
Flavours of Istanbul A Selection from Original 19th Century
Ottoman Recipes/Özge Samancı, Sharon Croxford

First edition in medya+ik, February 2007 (1 000 copy)

Publisher
Pelin Ulusoy Tepret

Editor-in-Chief
Eyüphan Erkul

Photographs
Sharon Croxford

Assistant Editor-in-Chief
Cenk Gültekin

Graphic Design
Meryem Alper

Printed and Bound in Ebru Grafik Basım Sanayi Inc.
Yeşilce Mah. Yunus Emre Cad. No:6
34418 4. Levent/İstanbul
Tlf: 0212 269 40 44

ISBN- 975-9185-10-5

PMP Publishing Group Inc.
Esentepe Mahallesi Kardeşler Caddesi No: 42
Esentepe 34394 İSTANBUL
Tlf: 0212 283 98 98 Faks: 0212 283 00 55
kitap@pmpyayincilik.com

www.medyatikyayinlari.com

Flavours of Istanbul

A Selection from Original 19th

Century Ottoman Recipes

ÖZGE SAMANCI
SHARON CROXFORD

ÖZGE SAMANCI

After completing her graduate studies in History at Boğazici University in 1998 in Istanbul, Özge has continued her PhD studies in Food History at EHESS, Paris. While preparing her PhD thesis on Istanbul's Culinary Culture of the 19th Century, she writes about Ottoman food history for academic journals and popular magazines. She has presented papers at conferences and symposiums in Turkey and abroad. Since 2003 she has been teaching food and culinary history in the Department of Gastronomy and Culinary Arts at Yeditepe University, Istanbul. In 2006 she opened the Istanbul Food Workshop with Sharon. Along with researching Ottoman and Turkish food history, Özge has spent years preparing and cooking food and is now sharing her knowledge and experience through lectures, practical classes and writing.

SHARON CROXFORD

After years of travelling to Turkey several times each year, Sharon moved to Istanbul in 2002. Originally from Melbourne, Australia where she studied to become a dietitian, Sharon moved to London, England in 1997. In the five years there she worked as a dietitian before training as a chef at Leith's School of Food and Wine in 2000. Following that she worked for several catering organisations and began lecturing at King's College University, teaching students about food and cooking, nutrition and dietetics. In 2006 she and Özge opened the Istanbul Food Workshop, a base from which she writes, photographs and teaches about food (and sometimes nutrition). She writes and photographs for Time Out Istanbul, Lonely Planet and other journals.

THANKS

Many thanks to everyone who has contributed to this book...

First of all we would like to thank Pelin Ulusoy Tepret for her warm-hearted approach and support.

We would also like to thank:
PMP staff for their valuable effort during the construction of the book;
Gözde Karakan and Vehbi Baysan for their help with English translations;
Özge's mother Hikmet Samancı for testing recipes and taking care of Sharon's daughter during the writing process of the book;
Pekin Samancı for his moral support;
Authors such as Mehmet Kamil, Ayşe Fahriye and Mahmut N. Tosun for their precious cookbooks and also all cooks and housewives who have brought these old recipes to life...

Contents

1- A sweets seller in Istanbul, 1860's.
2- Cookbooks in Old Ottoman Scripts.
3- Cook (Anonymous).

Cuisine of Istanbul in the 19th Century

Özge Samancı

The cuisine of Istanbul in the 19th century can be defined as the culmination of the Ottoman elite's cuisine that developed in the kitchens of the Ottoman palace and mansions of Istanbul's rich from the 15th to the end of 19th century. As the capital of the Ottoman Empire, Istanbul had the privilege of sourcing the best and most varied ingredients from each of its regions.[1] Beyond the food items and products of its immediate territorial limits, the kitchens of Istanbul also used foodstuffs from distant geographical regions of the Empire. During the 19th century rice was supplied from Egypt, butter from Kefe, salt from Walachia, mastic from Chios and honey from

Athens. Ottoman palaces and houses of the elite welcomed these ingredients and refined culinary techniques as symbols of their distinction and thus Istanbul's cuisine was 'created' or 'recreated' in this century. The use of these products resulted in the exclusive and rich variety of food typically seen in Ottoman palace cuisine. In addition, to distinguish themselves from the rest of society, the Ottoman elite developed and created new and different tastes from the 16th century through to, and especially during the 19th century. The abundant use of sugar and the great variety of desserts are two good examples of how the Ottoman elite's cuisine was distinctive. Common people ate deserts on occasions such as feast days, holidays and for special celebrations, but the Ottoman palace residents and notables ate sweets everyday. The cooks in the kitchens of the elite created different variations of one dish by

A meal in the house of the Ottoman elite

using different ingredients or techniques. There were more than ten types of helva and more than twenty kinds of sherbets described in Ottoman cookbooks published in the 19th century.

Another factor that played a critical role in the definition of the Ottoman elite's cuisine is Islam. The Muslim religion was practiced by most of the capital's population including the members of the ruling elite. Islamic rules about alimentation had an obvious influence on Istanbul cuisine. We can see from old Ottoman cookbooks that no recipes use alcoholic beverages or pork. Roasting or grilling meat until it is well done also comes from the Islamic rule of removing as much blood as possible by cooking such food very well. We can also see the effect of Christian and Jewish cuisines on Istanbul cuisine especially in the 19th century. For centuries Istanbul had been a house for all religions and therefore there were many Christian and Jewish people living in the city. There is no denying the effect these cultures had on the development of the cuisine of Istanbul's elite. According to cookbooks of the 19th century we understand that some dishes such as fish cooked in olive oil (*pilaki*), Priest's veal or fish stew (*papaz yahnisi),* sponge cake *(pandispanya*), salted bonito (*lakerda*) and walnut purée (*tarator*) originated from non-Muslim culinary traditions of Istanbul took their place in the cuisine of the Ottoman elite during that period. In addition, dishes that originated from Muslim culinary traditions such as savoury pastry dishes (*börek*), halva (*helva*), baklava and pilav were also integrated into the non-Muslim societies' cuisines. Many dishes were prepared and shared between the Muslim, Christian and Jewish communities' cuisines in Istanbul in the 19th century. This leads us to understand that the interaction between different cultural groups had an impact on the formation of an hybrid and rich cuisine that was enjoyed by Istanbul's elite.

We should not forget that Istanbul's cuisine in the 19th century was in part the product of a history going back to the first millennium in Central Asia. We recognize in the cuisine traces of nomadic culinary culture of the Turks from the 11th century. The influence of Medieval Arab, Persian, Seljuk and also Byzantine cuisines on Ottoman cuisine is also noticeable. After the conquest of Istanbul in 1453, the city became the capital of the Ottoman Empire. This made Istanbul the centre of culture, commerce and administration. At the same time Ottoman palace cuisine became important by symbolizing the characteristics of the imperial city.

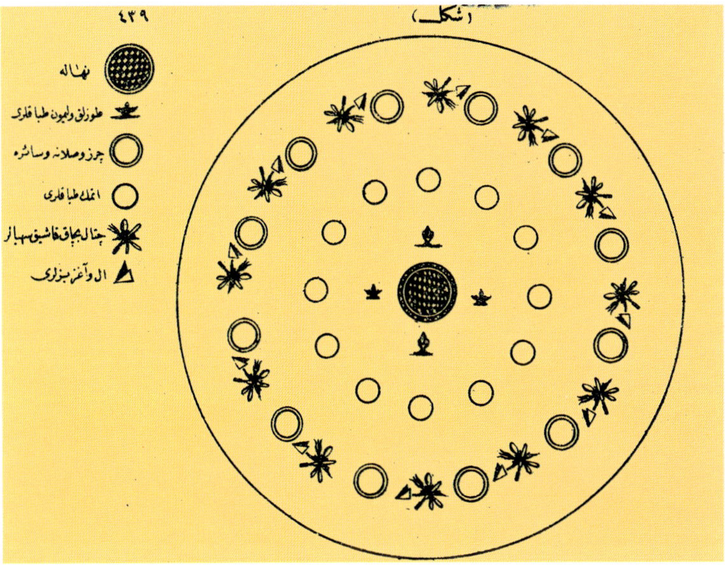

An example of a Turkish dinner table, *Ev Kadını.*

The Ottoman elite's cuisine developed and became refined throughout the centuries. New vegetables, fruits and spices that entered the cuisine of the Old World after Columbus's discovery of the New World in the 15th century played a major role in the development and change in Istanbul's cuisine. Among the new foodstuffs the most important and surprising story is that of the "tomato". It is remarkable to see that tomato, used in today's Turkish cuisine in abundance, has only existed in Istanbul's cuisine since the 1800's. Other vegetables native to the Americas that entered Istanbul's cuisine during the 19th century are vegetable marrows, green beans, red and green peppers, corn, Jerusalem artichokes and potatoes.[2] Another food item native of the Americas was turkey. Unlike new vegetables and fruits this animal established its place in the cuisine of Istanbul's elite during the 18th century. Turkey had been a part of the European elite's cuisines since the 17th century. Toward the end of the 19th century other new food items such as vanilla, paprika, cacao, allspice and a jelly extracted from fish (*balık-ı tutkal*) were used.

There are two main points that distinguish Istanbul's cuisine in the 19th Century from earlier centuries. One of them is the introduction of new foodstuffs originating from the America's mentioned above, and the other is the westernization of the Ottoman

Empire. This process influenced the culinary practices in the Ottoman palace and in the houses of Istanbul's notables from the 1850's.

Toward the end of the 19th century western culinary culture became a fashion, integrated into Ottoman culinary habits by some of the Ottoman elite who welcomed the idea of political and cultural reforms. Innovations were gradually realized in Ottoman eating habits and etiquette. The eating habits of Ottoman society had remained quite unchanged up until the 19th century. The meal was traditionally eaten around a low table (*sofra- sini*). People sat cross-legged on cushions and ate from the same plate. Spoons and fingers were the only instruments with which to eat. Knives and forks were unknown. Meals were not served in a special dining room, but people chose to eat wherever they wanted, the table was brought to them. During the second half of the century, a new style of eating became fashionable within the

An example of a Turkish dinner table in a girls school book.

Ottoman elite milieu. That of the European-style table manners, of having meals on a high dining table, sitting on a chair and using individual knives, forks, spoons, glasses as well as the use of European porcelain tableware. Parallel to the novelties adopted in the Ottoman culinary etiquette, European cuisine, especially French, started to influence the cuisine of Istanbul's elite during the second half of the century. We should note that the Ottoman elite initially welcomed European table etiquette as well as new European dishes in order to appear informed about European ways. The

Ottoman palace received its high-ranking foreign guests by preparing western style banquets and offering examples of dishes selected from French cuisine.[3] During this time European-style table manners as well as some European culinary techniques and dishes gradually became integrated into the Istanbul elite's cuisine. Ottoman cookbooks published during the last decades of the 19th century witness these changes. The Ottoman cookbook *Housewife* (*Ev Kadını*)[4] published in 1882-83 illustrates the growing interest of the Ottoman elite in European cuisine, especially French. In this book, some French recipes are described along with Ottoman recipes. New culinary genres such as sauces, pâtés, custards and cakes were described in this book.

Inside cover of Melceü't-Tabbâhîn.

Between 1844 and 1900 a series of Ottoman cookbooks were published in Istanbul. These cookbooks witness the richness and multi-coloured structure of Ottoman cuisine. Through these books we understand the cuisine of Istanbul's elite in the 19th century formed from the tastes of the past with foods and flavours more recently developed.

COOK BOOKS

In Ottoman food history, published documentation of Istanbul's cuisine began in the 19th century. The first cookbook named *Refuge of Cooks* (*Melceü't-Tabbâhîn*) was published in 1844.[5] According to Turgut Kut, specialist in the Ottoman cuisine, this book has been published several times and it has been a primary source for other cookbooks. After its initial publication in 1844, *Refuge of Cooks* was so popular that it was published again several times in the following years: 1849, 1856, 1859, 1867, twice in 1873 and in 1888-1889.[6] The author of the book, Mehmed Kamil, was a professor at the Ottoman medicinal school in Istanbul. In the introduction of the book, the author mentions that he decided to write such a cookbook in an attempt to revive old recipes that were forgotten or practiced incorrectly by the cooks of Istanbul. He complains about the current situation of Ottoman cuisine and mentions that the cooks did not know how to cook and wasted ingredients. Again, he remarks that while writing the book he referred to the old cookbooks and reports of people experienced in such matters.[7] The two main references used by Mehmed Kamil were manuscripts of recipes written in the

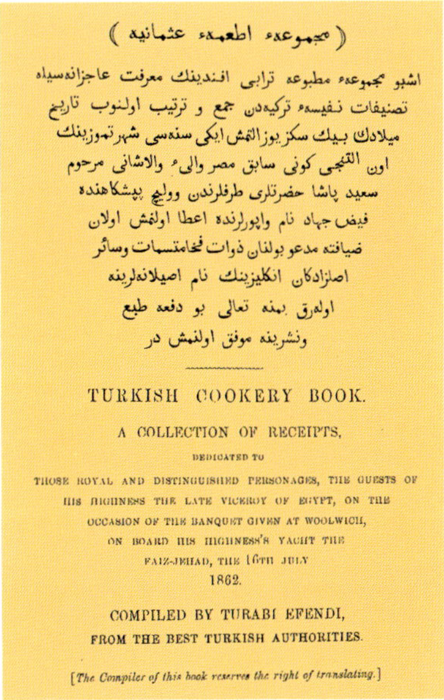
(مجموعهٔ اطعمهٔ عثمانیه)

اشبو مجموعهٔ مطبوعه ترابی افندینک معرفت عاجزانه‌سیله
تصنیفات نفیسهٔ ترکیه‌دن جمع و ترتیب اولنوب تاریخ
میلادك بیك سكز یوز التمش ایكی سنه‌سی شهر تموزینك
اون التنجی كونی سابق مصر والیٔ والاشانی مرحوم
سعید پاشا حضرتلری طرفلرندن وولیچ پیشگاهنده
فیض جهاد نام واپورلرنده اعطا اولنمش اولان
ضیافته مدعو بولنان ذوات فخامتسمات وسائر
اصلزادكان انكلیزینك نام اصیلانه‌لرینه
اوله‌رق بمنه تعالی بو دفعه طبع
ونشرینه موفق اولنمش در

TURKISH COOKERY BOOK.

A COLLECTION OF RECEIPTS,

DEDICATED TO

THOSE ROYAL AND DISTINGUISHED PERSONAGES, THE GUESTS OF HIS HIGHNESS THE LATE VICEROY OF EGYPT, ON THE OCCASION OF THE BANQUET GIVEN AT WOOLWICH, ON BOARD HIS HIGHNESS'S YACHT THE FAIZ-JEHAD, THE 16TH JULY 1862.

COMPILED BY TURABI EFENDI,

FROM THE BEST TURKISH AUTHORITIES.

[*The Compiler of this book reserves the right of translating.*]

Detail of cover, "Manual of Turkish Cookery".

18th century. The book includes a table of contents at the beginning and two hundred and seventy-three different recipes. *Refuge of Cooks* was important in many respects. It was the first example of a cookbook published in Ottoman society and it became a reference for other cookbooks published in Istanbul such as *New Cookbook (Yeni Yemek Kitabı)* in 1880, *Housewife (Ev Kadını)* in 1882 and *The Chef (Aşcı Başı)* in 1900. An Ottoman gentleman by the name of Türabi Efendi translated *Refuge of Cooks* into English in London in 1864.[8]

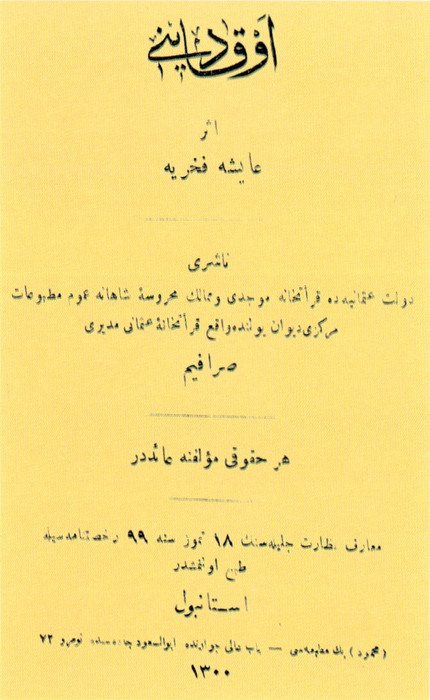

Inside cover, Ev Kadını.

Refuge of the Cooks contained thirteen sections: soups, roasts, stewed and fried dishes, pastry, milk and pastry desserts, vegetable dishes, stuffed dishes, pilavs, sherbets and compotes, salads and pickles. The book gives us detailed information about the ingredients used in cooking and about the cooking techniques of the time. *New Cookbook (Yeni Yemek Kitabı)*[9] is an anonymous book that was published in 1880/1881 in Istanbul. New recipes described in this book show us the influence of European styles of cooking in the cuisine of Istanbul's elite during the last decades of the 19th century. The name of this book, its content and the information that the author gives about why he wrote this book all show us the new trends that appeared in Istanbul's cuisine between the years 1850 and 1880. The author explains that he wrote this book to introduce new cooking styles compared to those of 30 years ago. He explains that the cookbooks that were previously written could no longer be used as a guide as there had been too many changes and developments in Istanbul cuisine. He indicates that the recipes in this book were the dishes that had been cooked in the mansions of Istanbul. *New Cookbook* contains 164 recipes. The book contained both familiar and new recipes.[10]

Another Ottoman cookbook published in 1882 illustrated the adoption of western culinary habits by Ottoman society. This book was written by an Ottoman woman

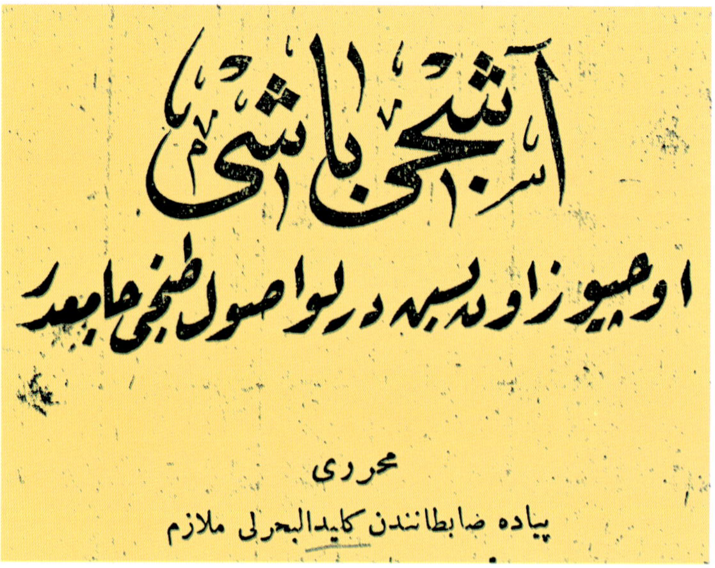

Detail of front cover, Aşçı Başı.

named Ayşe Fahriye and was titled *Housewife (Ev Kadını).* The author remarks in the introduction of the book that she wrote this cookbook in order to familiarize Ottoman ladies with the art of cooking, kitchen organisation and service style at the table. She mentions that the kitchen needed to be under the control of an Ottoman lady rather than cooks and servants who tended to run up vast expenses. In an attempt to introduce every aspect of food preparation, the author describes some basic principles of cooking, organization of the kitchen and storeroom, necessary tableware and utensils, service styles at the table, different sorts of meals, table etiquette, production and use of basic larder items, along with over eight hundreds recipes. Western style of service, western etiquette and western dishes were displayed in the book along with Ottoman etiquette, Ottoman dishes and service styles. The book also reveals some new concepts and terminology that were introduced into Ottoman culinary culture. The book was made up of thirty five sections; general remarks about cooking, soups and stocks, sauces, meat and fish gelatins, boiled and cold meats, egg dishes, roasts on skewers, grills, stews, fried dishes, meatballs (köfte) and sausages, oven roasts, stuffed dishes, vegetables, stewed and stuffed vegetables with meat, side dishes, fish and vegetable stews in olive oil (*pilakiler),* different types of sour and salted dishes, pâtés, pastry fillings, savoury pastries, pastas, pilavs, pastry desserts, puddings, sorbets, candies, jellies and ice-creams, jams, syrups, sherbets, compotes, pickles, salads and purées (*tarator)*, smoked fish, conserves, remarks about alcoholic beverages, clotted cream (*kaymak)*, yoghurt, cheese and clarified butter.

Engraving of a bakery in the beginning of 20th century.

Housewife differs in many respects from the first published Ottoman cookbook. In addition to the recipes that were described in *Refuge of Cooks*, *Housewife* includes many new recipes, most of which were examples of French cuisine. These recipes prove the Ottoman cuisine's acquaintance with new foodstuffs such as chocolate, vanilla, pineapple, tea and new cooking genres such as sauces, gelatins, side dishes, pâtés, custards and cakes during the second half of the 19th century.[11]

Another important cookbook that reflects 19th century Ottoman cuisine called *The Chef* (Aşçıbaşı) was published in 1900 by Mahmut Tosun. The author tells that he first understood the importance of cooking during his military service and so he decided to write this book. He researched old cookbooks and magazines and included 304 recipes in *The Chef.*

It is interesting that we do not see any measurements for ingredients of recipes in cookbooks published in the 19th century. At the time this was common practice and cooks would decide on the amount of ingredients according to their experience. The term "enough" or "enough of' an ingredient was used to describe the quantity to be used. In some recipes the use of old Ottoman measures such as *kıyye* and *dirhem* is seen.[12]

INGREDIENTS

Of the grains, wheat was consumed in the greatest quantity in 19th century Istanbul cuisine. The flour made from wheat was used in cooking different types of bread and several savoury and sweet pastries in Ottoman kitchens. Another important cereal was rice. It was used in cooking pilav which was one of the main dishes served at the Ottoman elite's table. As well as flour, starch, semolina and other cereal products were used in cooking desserts. Different kinds of vermicelli such as 'finest quality vermicelli', yellow vermicelli, white vermicelli and 'Istanbul's vermicelli' were used in cooking soups and pilavs.

Pasta was a luxury food item unlike nowadays. In the 19th century it was imported from Europe. Instead of pasta, *erişte* (a traditional kind of homemade macaroni), was used. The consumption of *bulgur* was limited in the cuisine of Istanbul's elite compared to the regional cuisines of Anatolia. Types of dried pulses used during this period were lentils, chickpeas, broad beans and haricot beans. Haricot beans, which are native of the Americas, began to be used in Istanbul's cuisine during the 19th century.

Apple seller, Sebah&Joaillier.

Clarified butter was the preferred type of fat used in 19th century Ottoman recipes. Most of the meat and vegetable stews, stuffed vegetables, savoury pastries, pilavs, desserts and even fried dishes were cooked in clarified butter. The fat obtained from the tail of mutton and suet was occasionally added in small quantities while preparing clarified butter. According to the Ottoman cookbooks olive oil was only occasionally used for frying and for seasoning salads. One explanation as to why olive oil was used so rarely in Ottoman cuisine is that the Ottoman palate was more familiar with the taste of animal fat. These latter fats were well-known in Ottoman culinary culture since its nomadic heritage on the steppes of Central Asia.

Milk, yoghurt, clotted cream *(kaymak)* and cheese were the dairy products consumed alone as well as in cooking in the 19th century. The types of cheese consumed were feta cheese (*peynir-i salamura*)[13], a yellow cheese *kashkaval*, Albanian cheese as well as cheese ripened in sheepskin *(peynir-i tulum)*. Milk was used for making yoghurt and puddings. Yoghurt was served as a side dish and sometimes used as a sauce with some dishes. *Kaymak,* served with desserts, was a highly valued food item and was consumed mostly by the elite.

Lamb and mutton were the favoured meats in Istanbul's cuisine of the 19th century. Mutton was always preferred and used more frequently in cooking than veal and beef in Ottoman cuisine at this time, as in previous centuries. Lamb was a delicacy in Ottoman Palace cuisine. Two ages of lamb were consumed, the newborn variety was known as *kuzu* and yearling lamb known as *toklu*. Every year, from the beginning of spring to the end of autumn it was customary to supply lamb to the Ottoman Palace, where it was distributed in greater or lesser quantities according to the rank of the recipient.[14] Chicken (*tavuk*), baby chicken (*piliç*) and turkey (hindi) were also used. We should note that consumption of chicken was more infrequent than that of mutton and that turkey was rarely eaten in the 19th century Ottoman Palace. Eggs were a popular food item used in preparing omelets and crepes (*kaygana*).

Engraving of a greengrocer and a 'Kaymak' seller in the beginning of 19th century.

According to the accounts of travelers and cookbooks of the time, fish and seafood were fashionable food items in Istanbul cuisine in the 19th century. Salted bonito (*lakerda*), caviar (havyar), fish roe (balık yumurtası), sardines (sardalya), salted and dried mackerel (*çiroz*) as well as other kinds of fish from the Marmara Sea were consumed by Istanbul's residents. Small portions of these dishes were served as *meze* to accompany alcoholic beverages. They were also eaten at meals after fasting during Ramadan. In today's Turkish culinary culture, it is rare to see caviar or fish roe at the table for the evening meal when people break their fast but in 19th century Ottoman cuisine it was commonplace to serve these items as appetizers.

Serving dish with cover, for pilav in 19th century.

Sweet dishes always played an important role in the culture of Ottoman cuisine. Sugar was an expensive product used in cooking sweet dishes so only wealthy people could afford the luxury. Common people used honey (bal), grape molasses (*pekmez*) and dried fruits in the preparation of desserts. Sugar, honey and other sweeteners were not only used in cooking sweet dishes but also in preparing sherbets, syrups and compotes.

Spices were used less frequently in the 19th century when compared to the 15th and 16th centuries in Ottoman cuisine. Analysis of the recipes shows that exotic spices like saffron, musk and coriander were not as common in the 19th century texts. The preferred spices in the 19th century were cinnamon and black pepper. Contrary to today's Turkish cuisine, cinnamon was mostly used in cooking savoury main dishes. It was even added to lamb, fish and chicken dishes. Cardamom, cloves, mastic, red pepper, allspice, cumin, sumac and saffron are other examples of spices used in cooking. Three types of salt were used; salt imported from Walachia, rock and lake salt. Rosewater (*gül suyu)* and orange flower water (*çiçek suyu*) were especially used in

A butcher in the beginning of 1900's.

cooking sweet dishes and sherbets. Nuts and dried fruits such as pine nuts, almonds or pistachios were also used as spices to add flavour to dishes such as pilavs, desserts and stuffed vegetables. Dried grapes, dried apricots, dried plums, figs, pears and sour cherries were used in cooking both sweet and savoury dishes, desserts and fruits drinks. Pokeweed and red dye extracted from the cochineal insect *(kırmız)* were used to impart colour to certain dishes, especially desserts and syrups. A fish-based jelly *(dutkal-ı balık)* also appears in this context, and suitably purified, was possibly used in making a fruit jelly called *elmasiye*. Lemon, vinegar and verjuice were also used in cooking sweet and sour dishes.

In the cuisine of Istanbul in the 19th century many fresh and cooked fruits are found. All kinds of fruits were used in making jam, sherbet, syrup, compotes and sweets dishes. Vegetables were also a big part of Ottoman cuisine. In summer eggplant and vegetable marrows were favoured, while some winter vegetables such as pumpkin, cabbage, spinach, leek and mallow were available towards the end of the warm season. Some other vegetables that we can see in the recipes of the period were; zucchini, gourd, okra, turnip, red and green tomatoes, cauliflower, cucumber, carrot, green pepper, onion, leek, cabbage, green bean, artichoke and even asparagus. In addition to wild herbs such as mallow, wild chicory, sheep's sorrel, parsley and dill, other greens used in the cuisine were purslane, lettuce and spinach. Vine leaves, hazelnut leaves and quince leaves were used in preparing stuffed dishes. Okra, a vegetable that entered Ottoman cuisine from Africa in the 17th century was used both fresh and dried in the 19th century. As mentioned previously, new vegetables such as tomatoes, corn, potatoes, green beans, zucchini, Jerusalem artichokes and green and red peppers were used in the kitchens of Istanbul from the 19th century.[15]

STYLE OF DISHES[16]

The five Ottoman cookbooks referred to include similar cooking techniques and culinary genres. *Housewife* and *New Cookbook* also included new dishes adopted from western cuisine. The traditional types of dishes in the cuisine of Istanbul in the 19th century were; soups, kebabs, stews and grills prepared with mutton, lamb, poultry and fish, meatballs (köfte), stews of vegetable dishes flavoured with meat, stuffed vegetables with minced meat or with spiced rice (*dolmalar)*, vegetables in olive oil (*zeytinyağlılar*), pickles, salads, egg dishes, pilavs, savoury pastries (*börek*), sweet pastries, helva, puddings, fruit desserts, jams, compotes, sherbets and cordials.

Ottoman cookbooks of the 19th century included few soup recipes when compared with the past. Soups were always prepared with chicken or meat broth and sometimes with pieces of lamb. The basic ingredients used in preparing soups were dried pulses and grains such as rice, chick-peas, and lentils. The basic thickener was made with lemon juice and egg yolk and was added to the soup just before service. Cinnamon, the favoured spice of the century, was also used as a seasoning in soups.

Dinner table at a mansion's 'harem' in Istanbul (1870's).

As mentioned previously mutton (and lamb) was the preferred type of meat used in dishes in 19th century cuisine. The use of veal was rare, found in just three or four recipes. Beef was only used in making dried and spiced meat called *pastırma*. Poultry and fish were also consumed. Offal such as liver, tripe and heads of mutton were also commonly used in Ottoman cuisine. The various meats were prepared using one of four main cooking techniques: roasting (*kebab),* griddling (*külbastı)*, stewing (*yahni)* and frying (*kızartma). Kebab* can be defined generally as a dry-cooking method. Spit roasting in front of a hot fire was one of the common ways of making *kebab.* Mutton, lamb, chicken, liver or fish were marinated with onion juice and occasionally with tomato juice or milk before being roasted on skewers. Salt, pepper and cinnamon were the main spices used in seasoning meat. Meat was also roasted in the oven or in a saucepan without the addition of liquid (*tencere kebabı*). Stuffed lamb baked in the oven (*içi dolmuş kuzu kebabı)* and mutton baked under a bowl (*tas kebabı*) are examples for this kind of roast. *Külbastı* was also a dry-heat cooking method. The meat for *külbastı* was prepared in thin slices from the best cut of mutton or poultry. Generally, after roasting on the grill, meat is placed in a pan with a little stock and is cooked until tender. Fish prepared in this way were grilled and served directly.

As mentioned above, stewing (*yahni),* like roasting was a popular cooking technique used in Ottoman cuisine in the 19th century. The Ottoman technique of stewing meat was quite different and much longer when compared to current culinary techniques. First the pieces of mutton were boiled for a few minutes in water. The scum that forms on the top was skimmed off. The meat was then removed from the pan and marinated in onion juice before being browned in clarified butter. Other ingredients such as onions, boiled chickpeas or dried fruits such as plums were sautéed. Finally, all the ingredients were simmered in the meat juice for at least one hour until the meat became very tender.

Another stew prepared at the time with fish, veal or beef was named "Priest's stew". While preparing these kinds of stews, the meat did not need to be boiled. Fish and mussel stews cooked in olive oil were named *pilaki.* Priest's stew and *pilaki* are examples of dishes originating from the

Cooking pan with cover in 19th century.

culinary culture of Istanbul's Greeks. Cookbooks published after the 1880's also include other kinds of *pilaki* made of vegetables such as tomatoes, leek, asparagus, mushrooms and pulses (dried beans). *Pilaki* became one of the culinary genres in Ottoman cuisine toward the end of the 19th century. Another method of cooking meat and especially fish was deep-frying, a method called "*tava"*. Pieces of mutton seasoned with salt, pepper and cinnamon were fried in butter. Small fish such as mackerel or anchovy were fried in olive oil. Sometimes mussels, pieces of mutton and lamb liver were coated in flour before being fried in olive oil.

Engraving of a traditional dinner table at the beginning of the 19th century.

Köfte was another specialty of Ottoman cuisine prepared with minced meat. These meatballs were prepared with minced mutton meat, grated onion and spices. *Köfte* were roasted, griddled, fried or braised. Egg dishes were also important in 19th century Istanbul cuisine and a special pan was used to fry eggs. Vegetables such as onions, spinach, artichoke and meat such as minced meat, *pastırma* and spiced sausage (*sucuk*) were some of the ingredients added to omelets. Vegetables or meat was sautéed in butter in a large pan, holes made in this mixture and eggs placed in these spaces.

Bread made from wheat flour was simply an accompanying food item at the table of the rich but a basic food item in the meal of the poor in Ottoman society during the 19th century. Flat bread without yeast made from thin sheets of dough (*yufka*) was consumed mostly in rural areas whereas raised bread like *pide* or *fodula* was produced in cities like Istanbul. The art of making bread rested within the milieu of the guild of bakers in the capital during the last epoch of the Ottoman Empire as it had throughout the centuries. Breads were differentiated by the quality and origin of the flour used in their preparation. The best kind of bread, prepared exclusively with white, pure flour of the highest grade, was devoted to the table of the Ottoman Sultan and notables. Ordinary varieties were consumed by the common people.

Savoury and sweet pastry dishes were of special importance in Ottoman cuisine during the 19th century. Wheat flour was used in the preparation of breads, savoury pastries (*börek)* and desserts such as baklava. Dough made from flour, water and salt formed the basis of the thin sheets of *yufka* used in the preparation of savoury pastries. According to the recipes of the 19th century a rich repertoire of *börek* made from simple dough, dough with butter and from flaky pastry were a part of Istanbul's cuisine. *Börek* was served as part of every meal at the elite's table. The basic method of preparing *börek* was to lay sheets of pastry in a tray and to spread a filling made from cheese, minced meat or chicken in the middle and then continue to lay sheets of dough on top of the filling. *Böreks* were cooked in the oven or on the stove. Small *börek* were fried in oil.

Spoons, handles are made with horn bone.

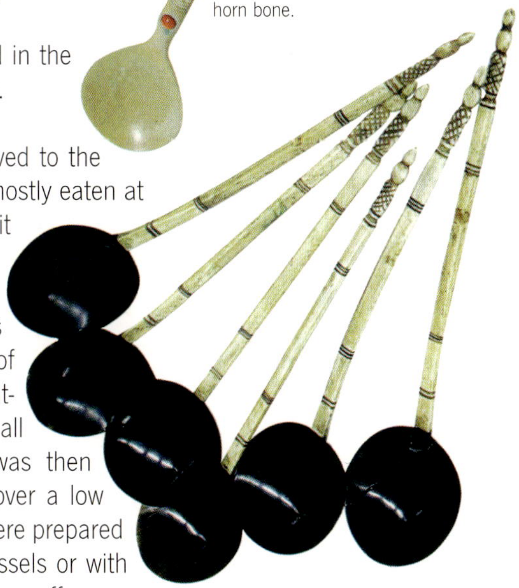

Along with *börek*, rice pilav was another dish served to the elite at every meal in Ottoman society. Pilav was mostly eaten at the end of the course and was accompanied by fruit compotes. Pilav made of cracked wheat (*bulgur*) was regarded as an inferior dish and not a part of the elite's culinary milieu. In Anatolia *bulgur* was more commonly consumed. The main technique of cooking pilav was to drop the rice into a pan of salted boiling water and to cook it on a low heat until all the water had been absorbed. Melted butter was then added to the pan and the pilav was simmered over a low heat for a further twenty or thirty minutes. Pilavs were prepared with pieces of lamb, chicken, bluefish (*lüfer*), mussels or with vegetables such eggplant and tomatoes. We also see saffron, mastic, black pepper and cinnamon among the spices used to flavour pilafs. In the 1880's pasta called *makaronya* was introduced into Istanbul's cuisine.

Ottoman recipes of the 19th century document a large range of vegetables dishes. Different kinds of vegetables were braised in clarified butter with pieces of mutton, onions and with the addition of a little water. Stuffing vegetables, leaves and even some fruits with minced meat, and braising them was another method used for cooking vegetables. *Bastı* was the name of the method of braising vegetables with pieces of meat in a little amount of water. Vegetables such as zucchinis, gourd, okra, eggplant or fresh beans were stewed with pieces of mutton and onions in butter. Verjuice or lemon juice was used to give a sour flavour to these dishes. Cinnamon, fresh mint, garlic and sometimes sugar were other condiments used in braising vegetables and in the recipes after the 1880's tomato juice was also used.

Another technique of cooking vegetables was called *silkme*. In this method pieces of vegetables such as zucchinis and eggplant were fried in butter, mixed with precooked pieces of mutton then simmered. Another type of braised vegetable called *musakka* consisted of fried vegetables simmered with minced meat instead of pieces of mutton.

Stuffed vegetables called *dolma* were prepared in two ways, with minced meat or with spiced rice. According to the recipes eggplant, marrow, cucumber, turnip, vine leaves and green tomatoes were stuffed with a mixture of chopped meat, rice, salt, pepper and onion. In some recipes, stuffed eggplant, marrow or cucumbers are

Gum mastic bowl.

Cyrstal sugar bowl.

coated in egg yolk before being fried in butter. They were then braised in a small amount of water with the addition of verjuice or sour plums. Vine leaves, hazelnut leaves, quince leaves, spinach or mallows were wrapped around a small amount of minced meat. Melon and pumpkin were two examples of savoury-style dolma with a sweet flavor. Another kind of stuffed dish was prepared with rice mixed with onion, salt, cinnamon, pepper, pine nuts, raisins, allspice and fresh herbs. These *dolmas* were called 'fake' as they did not include any meat. Olive oil was used in braising these 'counterfeit' stuffed vegetables in a small amount of water with sour plums or sour cherries.

Salads, pickles, spiced meats and seafood are just some of the appetizers described in the Ottoman cookbooks of the 19th century. These appetizers accompanied main courses and alcoholic drinks such as wine or *rakı*. It is important to note that the cookbooks of the time did not identify the term appetizer (*meze*) as a culinary genre. The understanding that these dishes were consumed as appetizers comes from other sources including memoirs describing details of the culinary practices of the time. The *meze* recipes for this book were selected after consulting these sources. According to the cookbooks of the time, salads were prepared with just one or two different herbs or vegetables. Mixed salads were quiet unknown. Lettuce, tomato, cauliflower, cucumber and chicory were used in preparing simple salads. The major salad dressing cited was made of olive oil, lemon juice or vinegar and salt. Aromatic herbs such as parsley, fresh mint and dill were used in salads. Another salad dressing used was *tarator*, a purée made of nuts, olive oil, lemon juice, salt, garlic and bread crumbs. *Tarator* was served with salads and also accompanied grilled fish or fried mussels. Salads made of seafood and fish such as shrimps, lobster, salted sardines and mackerel are also described in the recipes of the 19th century. Nearly every kind of vegetable as well as fruits such as melon, watermelon and unripe grapes were preserved in brine and sometimes in vinegar. Fish such as bonito were also preserved in brine. These dishes were served in the style we know as *meze*.

The large number of dessert and fruit juice recipes described in the cookbooks of the 19th century is impressive. Desserts held a very special place in Ottoman culinary culture. They were served during the celebrations of circumcisions, weddings and religious feasts as a symbol of joy. Desserts such as *helva* were also served during funerals in order to disperse the pain of the loss of a loved one. The various kinds of desserts described in the cookbooks of the time can be grouped as follows; sweet pastries soaked in sugar syrup (*baklava, kadayıf*), *helva*, puddings, fruit jellies *(elmasiye)*, fruit desserts, cookies, jams and candies. Fruit juices made of dried or fresh fruits such as compotes, sherbets and syrups are also included as varieties of desserts. As mentioned earlier, sugar was the basic sweetener used in making desserts in the 19th century unlike earlier periods, where honey and grape treacle (*pekmez*) were used. Toward the end of the century, the variety of desserts in Istanbul's cuisine was enriched and enlarged. Through cookbooks such as *Housewife* and *New Cookbook* we can observe that new western desserts such as custards, cakes and biscuits were introduced to Istanbul's cuisine.

Baklava, kadayıf, and *revani* are sweet pastries soaked in syrup. *Baklava* is made of thin pastry sheets sweetened with syrup. Varieties of baklava are created by using different fillings and different ways of layering and shaping. *Kadayıf* was a genre of dessert. It was made of vermicelli (*tel kadayıfı*), bread (*ekmek kadayıfı*) or of small circles of pastry (*yassı kadayıf*). The *kadayıf* were soaked in sugar syrup after being cooked either on a stove, baked in the oven or fried. They were stuffed or served with a nut filling or *kaymak*. Another category of desserts was made with yeast dough such as *lokma* which literally means "morsel". In order to prepare this dessert small pieces of dough are fried and then soaked in syrup. Cookies soaked in syrup were another kind of dessert made in Istanbul in the 19th century. Cake-type desserts, such as *revani,* are similarly sweetened with syrup. *Helva* is a dessert from ancient times. Originating in medieval Arab cuisine *helva* has been a part of Ottoman-Turkish cuisine since the first days of the empire in the 14th and 15th centuries. *Helva* is basically a roux mixed with a sugar syrup. Flour, starch and rice flour were used to make the roux and nuts such as almonds as well as rosewater are added for flavour. Semolina *helva (irmik helvası)* became popular in Istanbul cuisine in the 19th century. Recipes for the nougat-style of *helva* sold in sweets stores in Istanbul did not exist in the cookbooks of the time.

'Aşure' jug and 'aşure' cups.

Milk puddings were very popular desserts in Istanbul cuisine during the 19th century. Unlike today, rice pudding (*sütlaç)* was made without sugar. It was served with sugar sprinkled on top. Vanilla and cacao were rare and new ingredients used in making milk pudding. A blanc-mange style dessert *(tavuk göğsü)* made of shredded chicken breast is a medieval dessert that survived through the centuries to today. *Güllaç* literally meaning, "dish of roses", was another type of dessert popular in the 19th century. Thin sheets of dough made of starch were used in preparing different kinds of *güllaç*. The dough sheets were soaked in sugar syrup and flavoured with nuts, *kaymak* and rose water. "*Zerde*", another dessert, was made of rice, water and saffron. *Aşure* was a ceremonial dessert like *helva*. It was made of grains and pulses boiled in water, sweetened with sugar and flavoured with dried fruits, nuts and rose water.

Fruits jellies (*elmasiye*) made of gelatine extracted from fish were novel desserts in the cuisine of Istanbul in the 19th century. Fruits jellies prepared with starch were called *pelte*. Fruit desserts made of poached quince, apples, pears or peaches in syrup were also a part of the cuisine. Dried fruits such as plums, apricots and dates were boiled in syrup and served with nuts or *kaymak*. Jams made from all sorts of fruits and sometimes with nuts and edible flowers were served as a dessert in Ottoman cuisine. Recipes for the famous Turkish Delight *(rahatü'l-hulkum)* can be found in the cookbooks of the time.

BEVERAGES

Traditionally the consumption of alcohol was limited in Ottoman society. Theoretically alcoholic beverages were forbidden by Islamic law. Drinking alcohol during lunch or dinner was not common practice, therefore water and fruit juice became a very important part of Ottoman culinary culture into the 19th century. Istanbul inhabitants were exceptionally selective about the taste of water they drank. They were able to recognize the origin of different waters by taste. Snow and ice were still expensive items in the 19th century. Palace residents and notables had the privilege of using ice and snow in their beverages to keep than cool.

The three main types of fruit juices drank were compote (*hoşaf*), sherbet (*şerbet*) and cordial (*şurup).* In order to prepare a fruit compote, the fruit was boiled with sugar then mixed with pieces of fruit, previously set aside, before serving. Compotes accompanied pilavs and were served at the end of the meal. Sherbets and beverages made of fruit syrups were served as cold beverages during the day and also accompanied meals. Sherbets were made by kneading fruit with sugar then mixing with water. Cordials were a confection of fruit and sugar, boiled to a thick consistency, pushed through a sieve and served diluted with water. Plums, apricots, sour cherries, dried pears, blackberries, currants, oranges, pistachios, pomegranates, figs, almonds, lemons, quince and strawberries are examples of fruits and nuts used in making fruit juices. Syrups and jams were also made from petals of edible flowers such as roses, violets, jasmine and lilies.

Silver Coffee pot with Sultan's signature.

Although the consumption of alcohol was forbidden in Ottoman society by Islamic religion, some accounts of travellers and memoirs written in the 19th century witness Istanbul inhabitants drinking wine and *raki* in the taverns.[17] As we mentioned earlier these alcoholic beverages were served with *meze* such as salads, *tarators,* nuts, fruits and seafood.

The most popular hot beverage consumed at the time was coffee. Coffee had been known and consumed in Ottoman society since the 16th century. Unlike today tea was not a common beverage in 19th century Istanbul. It is worth noting that tea substituted coffee in the 20th century. The reason for this shift and the common consumption of tea in today's Turkey may be due to the production of great quantities in the North Sea region as well as its cheap price. Another hot beverage that was common in Istanbul in the 19th century was *sahlep*. *Sahlep* is a powder made of the roots of orchids. It was used mainly in the preparation of a hot beverage of milk and sugar that was served in large cups with cinnamon sprinkled on top.

The cookbooks published in Istanbul during the 19th century reveal the rich culinary repertoire of Ottoman traditions that were formed over the centuries meeting with recent European influences. In this book we introduce you to a selection of dishes chosen from the Ottoman cookbooks published between the years 1844 and 1900. You will find adaptations of old recipes alongside original ones in the following pages. We should note that the recipes for the dishes chosen are examples of traditional culinary genres that existed in Istanbul's cuisine in the 19th century. We preferred not to include western style dishes that had been integrated into the cuisine towards the end of the century. Among the fifty-nine recipes only one, Oven Baked Pasta (Fırın Makoronya), reveals the European taste of the time.

Holder.

[1] Mantran, Robert, *17. Yüzyılın İkinci Yarısında İstanbul*, Ankara: TTK, 1990, p. 167-201.
[2] Samancı, Özge, " Culinary Consumption Patterns of the Ottoman elite during the first half of the nineteenth century" in *Illuminated Table the Prosperous House*, Edited by Faroqhi, S. Neumann, Almanya: Ergon in Kommission, 2003, p. 161-185.
[3] Samancı, Özge, *Continuity and Change in the Culinary Culture of the Ottoman Palace in 19th Century* , Unpublished MA thesis, Istanbul: Boğaziçi University Social Sciences Institute, 1995.

[4] Ayşe Fahriye, *Ev Kadını*, İstanbul: Mahmud Bey Matbaası, 1300 (1882-1883).
[5] İlk Basılı Türkçe Yemek Kitabı *Melceü't-Tabbâhîn (Aşçıların Sığınağı)*, ed. Kut, Cüneyt., İstanbul: Unipro, 1997.
[6] Kut, Turgut, *A Bibliography of Turkish Cookery Books up to 1927*, London: Petit Propos Culinaire, PPC 36, 1990.

[7] Mehmet Kamil, *op.cit.* p. 21.
[8] Kut, *op.cit.* p.15
[9] *Yeni Yemek Kitabı*, İstanbul: 1300 (1882-1883).
[10] Samancı, Özge, "19. Yüzyıl İstanbul Mutfağında Yeni Lezzetler", *Yemek ve Kültür*, İstanbul: Çiya Publications, 2006, no. 6, p. 86-98.
[11] Ayşe Fahriye, *op.cit.*
[12] 1 *kıyye* equals 1.282 grams. 1 dirham equals 3.148 grams & 1 *kıyye* equals 400 dirhams.
[13] Named as white cheese (beyaz peynir) in today's Turkish cuisine.
[14] Samanci, Özge, "Culinary Consumption Patterns of the Ottoman elite during the first half of the nineteenth century" in *Illuminated Table the Prosperous House*, ed. Faroqhi, S. Neumann, Germany: Ergon in Kommission, 2003, p. 170.
[15] Samancı, Özge, " 19. Yüzyılda Osmanlı Saray Mutfağı" *Yemek ve Kültür*, İstanbul: Çiya Yayınları, 2006, sayı 4., p. 37-59.

[16] This section of the article is based on the information taken from the cookbooks of the 19th century.
[17] *Balıkhane Nazırı Ali Rıza Bey Eski Zamanlarda Istanbul Hayatı*, ed. Çoruk, Ali Şükrü, Istanbul: Kitabevi, 2001, p.179.

Cooking Techniques And Tips

Sharon Croxford

This section does not attempt to give detailed descriptions of all cooking techniques, just some used in the recipes that follow, with tips for preparing and cooking so that your bread rises, your pilavs are light and fluffy, your meat dishes are rich!

MAKING BREAD

Recipes for Bread (Ekmek), Flat Bread (Pide) and Sesame Bread Rings (Simit) are included. The method used for plain bread reflects the recipe in the original text and may seem a little obscure to practiced bread makers. The classic methods used for making plain bread include the following steps:

- Mix all ingredients,
- Knead dough until springy,
- Rise until double in size,
- Knock Back (knead again) to re-distribute gas bubbles,
- Prove until one-half times in size,
- Bake until browned on the outside and cooked in the middle.

In most bread recipes today, salt is added to the initial flour mixture. Salt gives bread flavour and also slows down the action of yeast. The plain bread recipe adapted for this book leaves the addition of a salt solution until after the first rise. This makes for some sticky work, incorporating the solution into the dough with extra flour, but the results are good. As there is no salt to retard the action of yeast in the initial dough, it will rise quickly. Care needs to be taken to ensure it does not rise too much and develop a strong yeasty flavour.

The recipes for flat pide and simit are interpretations of this classic method. Recipes for pide and simit do not exist in the historical texts, as the production of breads was the domain of bakers.

Regardless of the method used, follow these general tips to make good bread:

Mix

Use warm liquid 'blood temperature' for fresh yeast and even warmer liquid to activate dry yeast (43oC (110oF)). Heat activates dry yeast, causing it to reproduce and release carbon dioxide gas to raise the dough). Yeast can be mixed with liquid and a small amount of flour or sugar to 'sponge' before mixing with remaining dough ingredients. If substituting dry for fresh yeast, use half the quantity.

Knead

Knead using a mixer with a dough hook or by hand until the dough springs back to shape when pushed with a finger.

Rise

Allow the dough to rise until double in size in a warm, draught free place away from direct heat (as this will kill the yeast). Cover the dough with oiled plastic wrap to prevent cooling and drying out. Putting dough in the refrigerator at this time will slow the growth of yeast considerably and allow knocking back, proving and rising to be completed the following day. The flavour of the bread becomes more complex with this very slow rising.

Knock Back

Similar to kneading, however the purpose is re-distribute to the gas bubbles evenly and this step takes less time. Check the size and distribution of bubbles by cutting through the dough with a sharp knife.

Proving

Prove the dough in the same way as it rose. If using a bread tin or mould, place dough in the mould before proving. The size of the dough usually increases by one and a half however it will be ready when a light indentation remains after pushed with a finger.

Baking

Use a greased, warmed tin or tray. Place dough on the middle or slightly higher shelf if using a conventional gas or electric oven. Bake until it is browned on the outside and hollow when tapped on the bottom. Turn the loaf out of the tin and return to oven to 'dry out' if the bread does not sound hollow. Cool on a wire rack.

MAKING PASTRY

A wide variety of pastries exist in Ottoman and Turkish cuisine. 'Yufka', a thin fat-free dough, resembles the more commonly known filo pastry. After it is rolled out to the thickness required it is cooked briefly over a hot plate, before being used in savoury dishes. Yufka is used for the Filo Pancake with Spinach (Gözleme) and Cheese and Dill in Layered Pastry (Yufka Böreği). 'Coiled Baklava' (Sarıgıburma) again uses yukfa as the pastry, however in this sweet dish it is traditionally rolled out thinner than for the savoury dishes. The pastry used for the 'Turkish Pastry' (Türk Böreği) resembles a classic flaky pastry, with the addition of eggs in the initial dough.

The methods for making these two pastries differ significantly. Yufka is prepared in a similar fashion to bread, without yeast, and kneaded to work the gluten. Flaky pastry is not kneaded at all and the less the dough is handled the better!

Follow these tips for making yufka, or filo-type pastry:

- Knead dough until gluten is developed and springs back when pushed with a finger;
- Rest pastry between making and throughout the stages of rolling to let the gluten relax and allow it to be stretched with the rolling pin;
- Use lots of flour when rolling to prevent any sticking.

Following these tips will help produce good flaky and fat-containing pastry:

- Keep ingredients as cool as possible;
- Add any liquid all at once;
- Detrempe (beginning of pastry) in flaky or layered pastry needs to be a unitorm 'plasticine' consistency;
- Relax pastry between making and rolling to allow the gluten to rest;
- Refrigerate before baking;
- Bake in the top third of oven;
- Bake savoury pastry at a high temperature and sweet pastry at a slightly lower temperature;
- Cover edges with foil if they begin to get too brown;
- Bake until 'grey' areas dry, some pastries may need to dry out on bottom of oven.

PREPARING AND COOKING MEAT

Choosing the type of cut and fat content of meat will affect the texture and taste of a dish.

Many of the old recipes note the best type of meat to be used.

- For making 'köfte' (meatballs) lower fat minced meat should be used than when making meat-containing fillings for 'dolma' (stuffed foods).
- For cooking in a dry or very hot medium such as grilling or frying, more tender cuts with a higher fat content should be used.
- For cooking in a moist or low heat medium such as braising or stewing, tougher cuts may be used.

Browning meat is important for adding flavour (and colour) to dishes. Following a few simple steps will produce good results every time:

- Use a small amount of oil in the pan;
- Heat pan until very hot and just starting to smoke, then reduce heat;
- Season meat just before going into pan, not before;
- Make sure meat is dry;
- Do not overcrowd pan, brown small amounts of meat at a time and allow pan to return to temperature before adding more meat;
- Meat will 'release' itself from pan when it is sealed, so try not to push at it with a spoon!
- Water should evaporate when it is released from meat, the meat should not 'boil' in its juices.

Before starting to cook you may want to prepare your pan if it is non-stick!
...proving a pan
Pour about 1-2 tablespoons of oil in the pan, add a couple of teaspoons of salt and place on burner and allow to heat until just smoking; remove and very carefully wipe out oil and salt and use.

BRAISING VEGETABLES – IN OLIVE OIL OR BUTTER

Vegetables are a part of many dishes in Ottoman and Turkish cuisine, yet there are a vast number of dishes that rely on one main vegetable ingredient. These dishes will be cooked in either olive oil or butter. The olive oil dishes (zeytinyağlı), literally 'with olive oil', are prepared, allowed to cool and eaten cold. Dishes prepared with butter are served and eaten warm.

CLARIFYING BUTTER

Cooking foods in butter requires heating to high temperatures. Milk solids contained within the butter burn quickly and can detract from the overall appearance and taste of a dish (unless specifically required). Using clarified butter, where the milk solids are removed, prevents this. A quick and relatively easy way to remove or reduce the milk solids is to very gently heat butter until it is frothy but not burnt. Pour through a muslin cloth over a sieve into a bowl and use.

MAKING RICE PILAV

Rice is a sticky, starchy grain, but there are differences between grains. The best rice for making pilav are longer, fatter grains. Short-grain and cracked rice are often stickier and more suitable for desserts or dolma, where the starch that escapes adds to the dish. For pilav, rice needs to be washed and/or soaked to remove any excess starch before cooking, as the absorption method is used to cook the rice. When cooked and the water absorbed, small holes will appear in the surface of the rice. At this point the rice is allowed to rest and the recommended way to do this is to place a clean cloth between the pot and the lid and press down firmly. The rice will continue to soften, however any drops of moisture will be absorbed by the cloth and prevent the rice from overcooking. The finished pilav should be light and fluffy with the grains gently sticking together.

THICKENING

A variety of thickeners are used in both sweet and savoury dishes.
Flour or starch-based thickeners are used in soups and desserts. For the best results when using these thickeners follow these steps:

- Make a slurry by mixing flour or starch with appropriate quantity of cold water;
- If adding to a hot dish such as syrup, remove from heat, add a small amount of the hot liquid to the slurry and stir;
- Gradually add thickener to dish, stirring continuously;
- Return to heat and bring to a slow boil, them simmer for several minutes until flour or starch is cooked.

For egg-based thickeners:

- Beat egg yolk thoroughly with other ingredients such as lemon juice or cool broth;
- If adding to a hot liquid such as soup, remove from heat, add a small amount of the hot liquid to the egg mixture and stir;
- Gradually add thickener to dish, stirring continuously then serve.

Thickening meat and vegetable dishes:

- Thickening braised meat such as Braised Lamb with Prunes (Erikli Yahni) and vegetable dishes such as Carrots in Olive Oil (Zeytinyağlı Havuç) is a natural conclusion to cooking many dishes, with the amount of liquid added in the initial steps critical to the finished product. The contents of the dish should be cooked and the liquid reduced to an oily consistency without the need for extra reduction.

SUGAR SYRUPS

Sugar syrups are used extensively in desserts and drinks of Turkish and Ottoman cuisine. In general one standard recipe, made from a 2:1 ratio of sugar:water, with the addition of lemon salt (or lemon juice) will meet the needs for recipes requiring syrup. The syrup is gently simmered until the sugar dissolves. Large batches can be made up in advance and stored for later use. 500g sugar:250ml water with 1/2 teaspoon lemon salt should make 500ml syrup.

'KAYMAK' TURKISH CREAM

Kaymak is a rich, thick cream that can be rolled and sliced. It comes from water buffalo or cows milk. Many references cite 'clotted cream' as a suitable alternative. Home-made 'kaymak'-style cream can be made by bringing equal parts of full-fat milk and thickened cream to the boil then very gently simmering for 2 hours or until a skin forms. Leave to cool and refrigerate over night (for at least 12 hours) then skim off the skin and thick cream. You should be able to slice the cream and mould it between two spoons. Kaymak is about 60% fat.

Mezes

The recipes chosen in this section are a reflection of Istanbul, the choice of ingredients available and the variety of cooking methods used in the past and today. They are mostly vegetable and fish or seafood based and most are eaten cold. Slow cooking in olive oil, pureeing, pickling, frying, stuffing and poaching are some of the methods used.

Meze dishes are traditionally served in taverns and especially accompany alcoholic beverages such as rakı (aniseed flavoured drink similar to ouzo) or wine, which was the preferred drink during the Ottoman period. A selection of small portions are typically served. Tarator was a popular choice as a meze during the 19th century and was served with fish, seafood and vegetables. Pilaki originated from the non-muslim kitchens of Istanbul and was a type of stew of fish or seafood with olive oil.

Yoghurt, especially with garlic, oil and seasoning, can accompany dishes such as Fried Cauliflower and Carrot (Karnabahar Ve Havuç Kızartması) and Stuffed Zucchini (Kabak Böreği) and reflects the Turkish and Ottoman taste for the slightly sour but perfect accompaniment to savoury dishes.

Rice Stuffed Vine Leaves with Sour Cherries

VİŞNELİ YALANCI YAPRAK DOLMASI

Serves 4

INGREDIENTS

- 125g fresh grape vine leaves
- juice of 1/2 lemon
- 75ml (21/2floz) olive oil
- 150g (51/2oz) long grain rice, washed and drained
- 450g (3 medium) onions, chopped
- 15g (1/2oz) pine nuts
- 15g (1/2oz) currants, soaked if dry
- 1/2 teaspoon salt
- 1/2 teaspoon sugar
- 1/2 teaspoon cinnamon
- large pinch allspice
- 3-4 stems parsley, chopped
- 2-3 stems dill, chopped
- 400g (14oz) sour cherries (half de-stoned and pureed to make 100ml (31/2floz) cherry juice)
- 100ml (31/2floz) water

METHOD

1. Bring a large pan of water with lemon juice to boil.
2. Place vine leaves in water and simmer for 2 minutes, remove, refresh in cold water and set aside.
3. Heat olive oil in a large pan, add onion and pine nuts. Cook over low heat until transparent.
4. Add rice and continue cooking until opaque, stirring occasionally.
5. Add 25 ml sour cherry juice and 25 ml water and stir.
6. Cover and cook for 10 minutes until rice becomes slightly soft or rice absorbs water.
7. Add currants, salt, sugar, cinnamon, allspice, parsley, dill and mix.
8. Pick over the vine leaves leaving odd shaped ones to the side.
9. Lay the odd shaped vine leaves on the bottom of a large flat-based pan.
10. Take other vine leaves one at a time, remove the hard stem section of leaf, lay in your hand and place a spoon of rice mixture on the vine leaf (alternatively roll on a bench surface).
11. Fold bottom and sides of leaf across filling and roll tightly into a long thin shape about the size of your middle finger.
12. Place in the bottom of the pan with several cherries and repeat process with remaining leaves.
13. Place cherries over the filled vine leaves, inserting into any spaces.
14. Place a flat plate on top of the vine leaves and add remaining water and cherry juice.
15. Place lid on pan and cook over low heat until water is absorbed.
16. Leave in pan to cool.
17. Serve stuffed vine leaves with sour cherries.

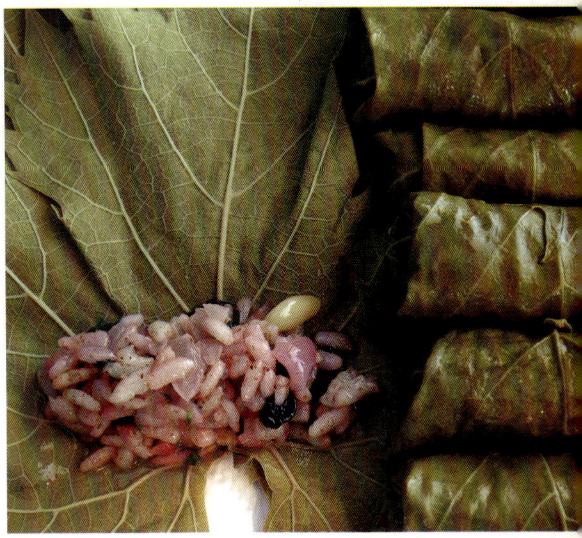

"VİŞNE YALANCI DOLMASI"
Mehmet Kâmil, Melceüt'-Tabbâhîn, p.69, no.5

Pureed Eggplant Dip

PATLICAN SALATASI

Serves 4

INGREDIENTS

- 750g (3 medium-large) round eggplant
- 2 large cloves garlic, pureed
- 30ml (1floz) olive oil
- 30ml (1floz) lemon juice
- 1/2 teaspoon salt

METHOD

1. Pre-heat oven to 180oC/350oF/gm4.
2. Pierce eggplants, place in oven and cook until skin begins peel.
3. Remove, cool and peel then pour over lemon juice immediately to prevent discolouration.
4. Place eggplant and garlic in a food processor and process until smooth.
5. Add olive oil and salt mixing thoroughly.
6. Serve.

Note *Grilling eggplant over charcoal gives a more complex flavour.*

"BADINCAN SALATASI"
Ayşe Fahriye, Ev Kadını, no. 743

Pureed Walnut Sauce with Cucumber

TARATORLU SALATALIK

Serves 4

INGREDIENTS

FOR CUCUMBER
- 200g (2 small) cucumber, peeled and sliced
- 1/2 teaspoon salt

FOR WALNUT DIP
- 55g (2oz) walnuts
- 20g (1/2 large slice) bread with crusts, torn in pieces
- 2 cloves garlic, roughly chopped
- 20ml (2/3floz) lemon juice
- 30-40ml water
- salt, freshly ground black pepper
- 15ml (1/2floz) olive oil

METHOD
1. Place cucumber in a bowl, add salt, mix thoroughly then set aside.
2. Place walnuts, bread, garlic, lemon juice, water, salt and pepper in a food processor.
3. Pulse until ingredients come together to form a paste.
4. While processor is running add oil and continue to process until desired consistency is achieved.
5. Mix tarator with cucumber and serve.

Not
1. Hazelnuts, sweet almonds or pine nuts can be used in place of walnuts.
2. Tarator is served as a side dish accompanying grilled fish, mussels, calamari, purslane or spinach, but is also a very tasty dip.
3. If you remove walnut skins tarator will be paler in colour.

HIYAR VE SEMİZOTU TARATORU
"Crack a pound of nuts or almonds, scald and skin them, then pound them in a stone mortar; add half a teaspoonful salt, three or four garlic peeled, and pound them well together with the nuts, then add the crumb of half of a French penny roll, previously soaked in water, and pound again all together till it forms a smooth substance like paste; then moisten it with half of a teacup of the best vinegar, or the juice of two or three lemons, and bring it to the consistency of cream with some water, stirring it all the time with a wooden spoon; then peel and cut in thin slices one or two cucumbers in a dish, season with a little salt and white pepper, and pour the sauce over; then pour one or two spoonfuls of the best olive oil over by degrees, and serve.
The leaves of purslain make a nice salad with the above sauce. Broccoli, cauliflower and the stalks of spinach, previously scalded, also make a good salad with the same sauce."
Türabi Efendi, A Manual of Turkish Cookery, no. 203.

Green Salad

YEŞİL SALATA

Serves 4

INGREDIENTS

- 80g (1 large) lettuce, washed and cut in three or four pieces
- 20 mint leaves
- 20 stems parsley, finely chopped
- 45ml (1 1/2 floz) olive oil
- 30ml (1floz) lemon juice
- 1/2 teaspoon salt
- small handful edible rose petals

METHOD

1. Place greens in a large bowl and mix.
2. Mix olive oil and lemon juice until frothy then add salt and mix.
3. Pour over greens, mixing to ensure every leaf is coated in dressing.
4. Garnish with rose petals and serve.

***Note** Sliced celery and watercress can be added for more texture and flavour.*

"YEŞİL SALATA"
Mehmet Kâmil, Melceü't-tabbahin,
p. 83. no.1

Salted, Dried Sardine Salad

SARDALYA SALATASI

Serves 6

INGREDIENTS

- 24 (1kg) dried, salted sardines
- 500ml (17 floz) good quality vinegar
- 90ml (3 floz) olive oil
- 45ml (1 1/2 floz) lemon juice
- 1/4 teaspoon salt
- large pinch teaspoon ground white pepper
- 4 stems parsley, chopped
- 4 stems dill, chopped

METHOD

1. Wash sardines in water to remove salt and leave to soak in large volume of water for 1-2 hours.
2. Rinse then soak in vinegar for 30 minutes.
3. Scrape away scales and trim heads.
4. Wash again in vinegar and lay on serving plate.
5. Place olive oil in a bowl and gradually beat in lemon juice until white and slightly foamy.
6. Season with salt and pepper and pour over fish.
7. Sprinkle with parsley and dill and serve.

SARDELYA SALATASSI
"Put as many as sardines as are wanted in a basin with some vinegar and let them remain in it for half an hour then scrape off the scales gently wash them in fresh vinegar and arrange them round the edge of a dish then put in the centre of it two or three handfuls of chopped parsley two or three tablespoonfuls of chopped onions and one or two dozens of olives all mixed together then put half a teaspoonful of salt in a basin with two or three tablespoonfuls of the best wine vinegar or the juice of two lemons and about half teacup of the best olive oil and beat up well with a wooden fork or spoon until it becomes like cream then pour it over the sardines and the parsley and serve."
Türabi Efendi, A Manual of Turkish Cookery, no. 204.

Pickled Beetroot

PANCAR TURŞUSU

Serves 4

INGREDIENTS

- 500g (6 small) beetroot, peeled and sliced
- 6 cloves garlic, with salt
- 20ml (2/3 floz) grape pekmez
- 200ml (7floz) good quality vinegar
- 100ml (3 1/2 floz) water of boiled beet

METHOD

1. Bring a large pan of water to boil, add beetroot and simmer until tender.
2. Remove and refresh in cold water, reserving cooking liquor.
3. Slice beetroot, mix with garlic, add pekmez and place in preserving jar.
4. Pour over vinegar and water of boiled beet, allow to sit for at least 3-4 hours.
5. Serve.

PANJAR TURSHUSSU
"Cut the stalks off and well wash four or five beetroots and boil them till tender; then peel and cut them into rather thin slices, and arrange them in a jar or glass bowl, with half of a pint of water in which they are boiled; then pound one or two cloves of garlic in a stone mortar with a little salt, add an ounce of powdered sugar, and half a pint of nice wine vinegar, stir well and pour it over the beetroots, then ready for use."
Türabi Efendi. A Manual of Turkish Cookery, no. 221.

Tomatoes in Olive Oil

DOMATES PİLAKİSİ

Serves 6

INGREDIENTS

- 1.5kg (7-8 large) tomatoes, peeled
- 120ml (4 floz) olive oil
- 400g (2 large) sliced onion
- 24-25 stems parsley, chopped
- 1 teaspoon salt
- 30ml (1 floz) lemon juice

METHOD

1. De-seed tomatoes over a sieve, preserving juice, then cut into 1cm slices.
2. Heat oil in large flat-based pan and gently cook onions then set aside half.
3. Spread onions across bottom of pan, cover with half parsley, lay half tomatoes over parsley then repeat layers once again.
4. Sprinkle with salt then pour lemon and reserved tomato juice over, cover and cook over a low heat until soft.
5. Allow to cool and serve.

Note *Add 4-5 cloves sliced garlic when almost finished cooking onions for another layer of flavour.*

"DOMATES PİLAKİSİ "
Ayşe Fahriye, Ev Kadını, no. 301

Stuffed Zucchini

PİYAZLI KABAK

Serves 4

INGREDIENTS

- 800g (8 small) zucchini, skins roughly peeled with serrated knife and cored (reserved)
- 150g (5oz) strong feta cheese, crumbled
- 5-6 stems parsley, finely chopped
- 5-6 stems dill, finely chopped
- 2 eggs, beaten
- 100ml (3 1/2 floz)olive oil
- water

METHOD

1. Chop flesh of zucchini, add cheese, parsley, dill and mix well.
2. Stuff zucchini with cheese mixture and dip in beaten eggs.
3. Heat oil in frying pan and fry stuffed zucchinis for several minutes, turning once or twice.
4. Place in large pan, add water until almost covered then bring to boil and simmer until zucchini tender.
5. Serve.

PİYAZLI KABAK

"Peel very thin seven or eight small size vegetable-marrows and take out the insides ; then stuff them with some nice cheese, grated and mixed with one or two tablespoonfuls of mint chopped; then beat up three or four eggs, in which dip the vegetable-marrows, and fry them a nice brown in hot fresh butter; then take them out and place them in a stewpan, cover them with broth set the pan on a charcoal fire, and let it boil gently, until the liquor is nearly absorbed; then dish up and serve."

Türabi Efendi, A Manual of Turkish Cookery, no. 109.

Fish in Olive Oil

BALIK PİLAKİSİ

Serves 6

INGREDIENTS

- 60ml (2 floz) olive oil
- 200g (1 large) onion, sliced
- 500g (18oz) white flesh fish, cut in pieces
- 400g (2 large) tomatoes, peeled and cut in quarters
- 12 garlic cloves, sliced
- 15 stems parsley, chopped
- 100ml (3 1/2 floz) good quality vinegar
- 1/2 teaspoon salt
- 1/2 teaspoon freshly cracked black pepper
- 1/2 teaspoon ground cinnamon

METHOD

1. Heat half oil in large flat-based pan and gently cook onions then set aside.
2. Spread fish across bottom of pan, cover with onions, tomatoes, garlic, parsley, vinegar, remaining olive oil, vinegar, salt, pepper and cinnamon.
3. Cover and cook over a low heat until fish tender.
4. Allow to cool and serve.

ADİ BALIK PİLAKİSİ
Mehmet Tosun, Aşçı Başı, no.75

Carrots in Olive Oil

ZEYTİNYAĞLI HAVUÇ

Serves 4

INGREDIENTS
- 700g (1 1/2 lb) baby carrots, peeled
- 90ml (3floz) olive oil
- 400g (2 large) onion, sliced
- 10 cloves garlic, sliced
- 2 teaspoons salt
- 1/4 teaspoon freshly cracked black pepper
- 300ml (1/2 pint) water

METHOD

1. Cut carrots lengthways from just below the top to the point then repeat to form four points.
2. Heat olive oil and sauté onions gently until almost softened then add garlic and cook a further few minutes.
3. Add carrots and stuff with onions and garlic.
4. Add salt, pepper and water then bring to boil, reduce heat and simmer with lid on until carrots begin to soften.
5. Continue to cook until carrots tender and remaining juice oily in consistency.
6. Allow to cool and serve.

Note: Large carrots can be shaped into baby-sized carrots as below.

ZEYTİNYAĞLI HAVUÇ
Ayşe Fahriye, Ev Kadını, no. 263.

Shrimp Salad

TEKE SALATASI

Serves 4

INGREDIENTS

- 1kg (2.2lb) raw shrimps
- 6-8 stems parsley, chopped
- 60ml (2floz) olive oil
- 20ml (2/3 floz) lemon juice
- 1/2 teaspoon salt

METHOD

1. Wash shrimps and place in a large pan of water.
2. Bring to boil and simmer for one or two minutes.
3. Remove head, shell and place in a bowl.
4. Add remaining ingredients, mix and serve.

TEKE SALATASSI
Take off the skins and the heads of three or four dozen prawns, arrange them in a dish with a handful or two of picked parsley, sprinkle a pinch or two of salt over, with the juice of one or two lemons, and two or three tablespoonfuls of best oil, and serve.
Türabi Efendi, A Manual of Turkish Cookery, no. 209.

Fried Cauliflower and Carrot

KARNABAHAR VE HAVUÇ KIZARTMASI

Serves 4

INGREDIENTS

- 200g (1/4 medium) cauliflower, cut into florets
- 200g (2 medium) carrots, peeled and cut into flat batons
- 2-3 eggs, beaten
- 140g (5oz) flour, seasoned with salt and finely ground white pepper
- 200ml (7floz) vegetable oil, for frying
- salt

METHOD

1. Drop cauliflower into a large pan of salted boiling water for a few minutes until just tender.
2. Drain and refresh in cold water.
3. Repeat with carrots.
4. Dip carrot and cauliflower in egg then coat in flour.
5. Heat oil in a large pan.
6. Drop carrot and cauliflower, a few pieces at a time, into the oil and fry until golden.
7. Drain on paper towel and sprinkle lightly with salt.
8. Serve hot.

Note *Serve with a mixture of 200g yogurt and 4-5 pureed garlic cloves.*

KARNABAHAR TAVASI
Ayşe Fahriye, Ev Kadını, no. 152.

Soups

Soups are a very important part of Turkish culinary culture. The four recipes that follow use different types of main ingredients (filled pasta dumplings, chickpeas, vegetables and chicken) with three of the original recipes relying on meat (lamb) as a flavouring and for stock. This is typical of the soup recipes of the time, where meat was used widely across dishes but not as the primary ingredient in the dish. Vegetable soup, therefore, contains a small amount of lamb although this can be omitted. We opted for a vegetable based stock in the recipe for the chickpea soup. Chickpea soup is the most traditional recipe known from the 18th century whilst the others reflect influences from the multicultural characteristics of the Ottoman Empire.

Soup with Stuffed Pastries

KULAK ÇORBASI

Serves 4

INGREDIENTS

FOR PASTRY

- 1 egg
- 55ml (2floz) meat stock
- 175g (6oz) flour
- 2 pinches salt

FOR FILLING

- 10g (1/3 oz) butter
- 100g (1/2 large) finely chopped onion
- 100g (3 1/2 oz) minced lamb
- 10 stems parsley, chopped
- salt
- pepper

FOR SOUP

- 1600ml (2 1/2 pints) meat stock
- 40g (1 1/2 oz) flour

FOR GARNISH

- 20g (3/4 oz) butter
- 1/4 teaspoon paprika

METHOD

1. Mix egg and stock together.
2. Sift flour into bowl, make well in centre, pour in egg and mix until a soft dough forms.
3. Rest for 10-15 minutes.
4. Meanwhile sauté onion in butter over medium heat until just brown.
5. Add meat, parsley, salt and pepper and continue to cook for several minutes, stirring to incorporate ingredients then set aside.
6. Divide pastry in two and roll out to 30cm(12inch) squares then cut into 2.5cm (1inch) squares.
7. Take a pinch of meat filling, lay in middle of pastry square then fold the bottom then sides from the corners into the middle.
8. Press firmly and slightly twist the remaining opening, patting with a little flour to stop pastries sticking to each other.
9. Bring stock for soup to the boil, add pastries and simmer until they rise to the top.
10. Make a paste with flour and a small amount of water, adding stock until a slurry forms.
11. Add slurry to soup and simmer for several minutes to thicken.
12. In another small pan melt butter and sauté paprika.
13. Serve soup with butter and paprika drizzled over top.

Note *The literal translation of kulak çorbası is ear soup!*

"KULAK ÇORBASI"
Ayşe Fahriye, Ev Kadını, no. 37 .

Pureed Chickpea Soup

NOHUT ÇORBASI

Serves 6

INGREDIENTS
- 400g (14oz) chickpeas, soaked overnight then boiled until tender
- 2.5 litres (4 1/4 pints) water
- 4 parsley stems
- 2 bay leaves
- 100g (1 small onion), cut in half, skin on, washed
- 50g (1/2 medium carrot), peeled
- 2 teaspoons salt
- 1/2 teaspoon freshly cracked black pepper
- 30g (1oz) butter, melted
- 1 large pinch saffron

METHOD

1. Remove the outer husks of the chickpeas and place in a large pan.
2. Add remaining ingredients and bring to the boil then simmer for 10 minutes.
3. Remove parsley, bay leaves, onion and carrot and continue to simmer until chickpeas soft.
4. Add saffron to melted butter and gently warm.
5. Puree chickpeas with food processor or hand blender and serve with butter and saffron drizzled on top.

NOKHUD CHORBASİ
"Scald a sufficient quantity of chick peas, and remove the pods or skins; then put again into the same water, and boil until quite soft; then drain and mash them with the back of a wooden spoon, and pass them through a sieve into a stewpan; then moisten it as much broth as the quantity of soup wanted; set it on the fire and let it simmer until reduced to a nice consistency; then pour it in a tureen, sprinkle a little cinnamon over, and serve with toasted or fried bread in small dice."
Türabi Efendi, A Manual of Turkish Cookery, No. 6.

Vegetable Soup

SEBZE ÇORBASI

Serves 4

INGREDIENTS

- 30g (1oz) butter
- 200g (2 large) carrots, grated
- 200g (2 medium) leek, white part sliced
- 150g (1 small) celeriac, chopped
- 150g (1 medium) turnip, chopped
- 300g (2 medium) onions, quartered and sliced
- 100g (3 1/2 oz) lean lamb, chopped in 1.5cm cubes
- 4 stems parsley, chopped
- 1500ml (2 1/2 pints) vegetable stock
- 1 tablespoon flour
- 1 egg yolk, beaten
- 15ml (1/2floz) lemon juice

METHOD

1. Melt butter in large pan and brown vegetables.
2. Meanwhile, place meat in small pan, cover with water and bring to the boil, removing scum as it surfaces then drain.
3. Add parsley, meat and stock to vegetables, bring to boil, reduce heat and simmer until meat tender.
4. Mix flour with enough water to make a smooth slurry, add some broth from the soup, mix then pour into soup and stir.
5. Continue to cook for several minutes until flour cooked then remove from heat
6. Beat egg yolk with lemon juice and just before serving add some broth to egg and mix.
7. Pour into soup, stir and serve.

Note *For a vegetarian soup, lamb may be omitted and seasoning adjusted accordingly.*

"SEBZE ÇORBASI"
Ayşe Fahriye, Ev Kadını, no. 39.

Circassian Soup

ÇERKEZ ÇORBASI

Serves 4-6

INGREDIENTS

- 1.5kg (1 medium) chicken, washed
- 200g (2 medium) sweet green peppers, deseeded and chopped
- 200g (2 medium) sweet red peppers, deseeded and chopped
- 300g (10 1/2 oz) cooked corn kernels, rinsed and drained
- 1 teaspoon salt
- 1/2 teaspoon freshly cracked black pepper

METHOD

1. Place chicken in a large pan, cover with water, bring to boil then simmer until cooked, removing any scum that forms on the surface.
2. Remove chicken, reserving stock and pull meat from bones, shredding into small pieces.
3. Return to a clean pan with the stock and peppers then bring to boil again.
4. Simmer until peppers almost tender, add corn and continue to simmer until soft.
5. Add salt and pepper, stir and serve.

"ÇERKEZ ÇORBASI"
Ayşe Fahriye, Ev Kadını, no. 42.

Breads and Savoury Pastries

The breads chosen reflect three breads of the time that remain popular today. Bread (Ekmek) is common at any mealtime and Sesame-coated Bread Rings (Simit) for a snack on the run. The Flat Bread (pide) we have included is the long, flat bread dusted with nigella seeds eaten with meze and main dishes especially during Ramadan, rather than the fast food pide with toppings similar to pizza. Recipes for simit and pide are not recorded in the recipes books and cooking references of the 19th century as they were not baked at home. It was the local bakers' duty to prepare such breads and these recipes have been passed from baker to baker and continue to remain a part of this tradition. The recipes included are interpretations of known recipes coupled with knowledge of current methods.

Two of the savoury pastry dishes are made with 'yufka' which resembles the commonly known filo pastry. Yufka is made from a fat-free dough and rolled out to large circles of varying thickness, depending on the dish it will be used for as well as the skill of the 'pastry chef'! Yufka is cooked briefly on a hot, slightly convex pan, called a 'saç' in Turkish, before being used for savoury dishes. For sweet dishes such as baklava, the pastry might be thinner and is used fresh. In both the 'Cheese and Dill in Layered Pastry (Yufka Böreği) and the Filo Pancake with Spinach (Gözleme) commercially produced yufka or filo pastry may be used. In both these dishes the fillings used may also be changed.

Flat Bread

PİDE

Makes 2

INGREDIENTS

FOR SPONGE

- 20g (2/3 oz) fresh yeast
- 1/2 teaspoon sugar
- 20g (2/3 oz) flour
- 100ml water

FOR BREAD

- 250g (8oz) strong flour
- 1 teaspoon salt
- 30ml (1 floz) olive oil

FOR GLAZE

- 1 beaten egg yolk
- 1 teaspoon nigella seeds

METHOD

1. Mix ingredients for sponge in a large bowl and stand for 20 minutes.
2. Sift flour and salt, add to sponge with olive oil and mix well.
3. Knead on lightly floured surface until smooth and elastic.
4. Place in lightly oiled bowl, cover with a clean cloth, leave in a warm place and allow to double in size.
5. Preheat oven to 220oC/425oF/gm7.
6. Knock back dough, divide in two, knead until smooth then let rest for 5-10 minutes.
7. Shape into long ovals, pressing to flatten then leave to prove for another 5-10 minutes.
8. Lay on hot oven tray, brush with egg yolk, sprinkle with nigella seeds and bake for 8-10 minutes.
9. Remove and allow to cool on a wire rack before serving.

Sesame Bread Rings

SİMİT

Makes 8

INGREDIENTS

FOR SPONGE

- 20g (3/4 oz) fresh yeast
- 1/4 teaspoon sugar
- 60ml (2floz) water

FOR BREAD

- 600g (1lb5oz) strong white flour
- 1 1/2 teaspoons salt
- 260ml (9 floz) water

FOR POACHING

- 300ml (1/2 pint) grape pekmez
- 900ml (1 1/2 pints) water

FOR COATING

- 200g (7oz) sesame seeds

METHOD

1. Mix ingredients for sponge in a large bowl and stand for 20 minutes.
2. Sift flour and salt, then add sponge and remaining water ensuring all yeast is incorporated, mix to form a soft dough.
3. Knead on lightly floured surface until smooth and elastic (approx. 10 minutes).
4. Place in lightly oiled bowl, cover with a clean cloth, leave in a warm place and allow to double in size.
5. Knock back dough, divide in eight, knead until smooth then let rest for 5 minutes under a damp cloth.
6. Roll into 25cm lengths then join ends to from a ring, sticking with water if necessary.
7. Leave covered with a damp cloth on a floured board until they increase in size by one and a half.
8. Preheat oven (with oven tray) to 200oC/400oF/gm6.
9. Bring pekmez and water to boil in large flat-based pan then reduce to simmer.
10. Lower each simit into pekmez and poach gently for 2 minutes on each side.
11. Remove, coat in sesame seeds and place back on board.
12. Lay simit on pre-heated oven tray and bake for 12-15 minutes.
13. Allow to cool slightly before serving.

Notes

1. Special sesame seeds are used for making simit commercially.
2. Simit are best eaten fresh.

Bread

EKMEK

Makes 2

INGREDIENTS
- 250ml (9floz) lukewarm water
- 550g (1 1/4 lb) strong white flour
- 40g (1 1/2oz) fresh yeast
- 2 teaspoons salt dissolved in small amount of water
- 1 teaspoon sesame or nigella seeds
- 1 egg yolk, beaten

METHOD
1. Mix 220ml of the water and 450g flour together.
2. Dissolve yeast in remaining water.
3. Add yeast to flour and knead until smooth and elastic.
4. Leave to rise until it doubles in size.
5. Knock back and add salt solution and remaining flour, kneading well to incorporate.
6. Shape as desired and leave to prove.
7. Preheat oven to 200oC / 400oF / gm6.
8. Glaze with egg yolk and sprinkle with sesame or nigella seeds.
9. Bake for 20 minutes or until browned and hollow sounding when tapped on the bottom.

"ETMEK"
Ayşe Fahriye, Ev Kadını, no. 379.

Cheese and Dill in Layered Pastry

YUFKA BÖREĞİ

Makes 1 (25cm tray)

INGREDIENTS

FOR DOUGH

- 170g (6oz) flour
- 1/4 teaspoon salt
- 90-100ml (3floz) water

FOR FILLING

- 120g (4oz) white cheese, crumbled
- 2-3 stems dill, chopped
- 1 egg and 1 white (from glaze), beaten

EGG WASH FOR PASTRY LAYERS

- 1 egg, beaten
- 90ml (3 floz) water
- 30g (1oz) butter, melted

FOR GLAZE

- 1 egg yolk, beaten and strained

METHOD

1. Sift flour and salt, make a well in the centre and add water.
2. Mix with a large knife until soft dough forms, knead lightly until smooth then rest for 10-15 minutes.
3. Meanwhile mix ingredients for filling and pastry layers in separate bowls and set aside.
4. Take pastry and divide into 6 walnut sized pieces then roll out into circles on a floured board until a couple of millimetres thick and larger than tray.
5. Heat a tray (or frying pan if large enough) until very hot and cook each pastry sheet briefly on both sides.
6. Preheat oven to 200oC/400oF/gm6.
7. Grease tray with butter and lay first sheet of pastry in waves on base, leaving draped over sides.
8. Using a large pastry brush apply egg wash liberally over first sheet.
9. Drape second sheet, again in waves across first, ensuring all pastry is within tray.
10. Repeat steps 8,9 with third sheet.
11. Lay filling across pastry then repeat draping pastry and egg washes three times, using all egg wash.
12. Fold excess pastry from sides of tray across the top and glaze with egg yolk.
13. Bake for 20 minutes until golden brown and pastry cooked on bottom.
14. Allow to cool then cut into slices and serve.

Note *Pre-prepared yufka may be used and if not available filo pastry is a reasonable substitute.*

YUFKA BUREGHİ
"Place two or three pounds of flour on the table-dresser, or in a pan, make a hole in the center, put in a little salt, and sufficient water, and stir it well up with a wooden spoon; then throw a little flour over, and knead well with the hands until it forms a nice paste; then divide it into small pieces (say eight or ten) and roll them out thin about the thickness of a sixpence, and the size of a baking-tin intended for laying them in. Then bake them soft, one by one, on a hot stove (such as crumpets are baked on), or a baking sheet which is placed over a trivet on a wood or charcoal fire. When done nicely on both sides, beat up two or three eggs in a basin, with a teacup of broth, then grease the baking-tin with fresh butter, and lay in half the pieces of past one over the other, sprinkling some of the beaten-up egg; and fresh butter between each one with a quill or a paste-brush; then lay some fried minced meat all over, half an inch thick, which is prepared from raw mutton or beef, and then cover it with the remaining of pieces of paste, as above; egg and butter over, place it in the oven until nicely browned on both sides. When done, cut it in diamonds, or any other shape, dish up, and serve hot. If a little finely chopped onions, stewed in fresh butter, be added to the fried minced meat, it will freshen it, and improve the flavor of it.
Cheese may be used instead of minced meat if preferred, thus: grate some nice cheese, then add to it a handful of fennel, chopped fine, one or two raw eggs, and a little pepper and salt; mix them well together, and lay it between the pastes as above."
Türabi Efendi. A Manual of Turkish Cookery. No. 76.

Turkish Pastry

TÜRK BÖREĞİ

Makes 2

INGREDIENTS

FOR DOUGH

- 450g (1lb) flour
- 1/4 teaspoon salt
- 2 eggs, beaten
- 200ml (7floz) water
- 300g (10 1/2 oz) butter, chopped and kept cool

FOR FILLING

- 300g (10 1/2 oz) minced lamb
- 200g (1 large) chopped onion
- 30g (2oz) pine nuts, toasted
- 30g (2oz) currants
- 1 teaspoon freshly cracked black pepper
- 1 teaspoon cinnamon
- 10 stems parsley, chopped

FOR GLAZING

- 1 egg yolk, beaten

METHOD

1. Sift flour and salt, make a well in the centre and add eggs and water.
2. Mix with a large knife until soft dough forms, knead lightly until smooth, cover and rest in refrigerator for 10-15 minutes.
3. Meanwhile brown meat in a frying over a medium-high heat then add onions and continue to cook for several minutes.
4. Add pine nuts, currants, salt, pepper, cinnamon and parsley then cook a further few minutes.
5. Divide dough in two and roll out into 15 x 25cm rectangles.
6. Place one-sixth of butter over bottom two-thirds of pastry, fold top-third down and bottom-third up, turn one-quarter and repeat then wrap in a freezer bag and rest in refrigerator for 10 minutes.
7. Roll pastry to same size and fold once as above without addition of butter then twice with addition of butter then rest again for 10 minutes.
8. Repeat rolling, folding and resting in step 7.
9. Preheat oven to 200oC/400oF/gm6.
10. Roll pastry out to 25 x 60cm rectangle and cut in two.
11. Place half in the base of a greased 25cm shallow tray, spread meat filling over and cover with remaining pastry, trimming edges.
12. Glaze with egg yolk and bake for 20 minutes until golden brown.
13. Repeat steps 10-12 for second börek.
14. Serve.

Note

1. Good pastry is made in a cool environment. If possible refrigerate the prepared pastry for 10-15 minutes before baking.
2. Pre-prepared flaky pastry sheets may be used.

TURK BUREGHI
"Put on the dresser a pound of flour , make a hole in the center, in which put a teaspoonful of salt, break in two eggs, mix all together; then add sufficient water, and form it a softish flexible paste, divide into tow, and roll them out to the size of the baking-tin you intend to use; then sprinkle some melted fresh butter over, and fold over the edges of the paste so as to hide the butter, throw a little flour both under and over, and roll tem out again as before, repeat the same five or six times more; then butter the baking-tin, in which lay one of the two pieces of paste; then lay any preparation you choose all over it, half an inch thick, and cover it with the other paste; then make about fifteen deep holes in the paste here and there with the point of a knife, and bake it a nice brown on both sides. When done, cut it in diamonds, dish up tastefully, and serve hot."
Türabi Efendi, A Manual of Turkish Cookery, no. 83.

Filo Pancake with Spinach

ISPANAKLI GÖZLEME

Makes 8 small

INGREDIENTS

FOR DOUGH

- 170g (6oz) flour
- 1/4 teaspoon salt
- 90-100ml (3floz) water

FOR FILLING

- 15g (1/2 oz) butter
- 80g (1/2 medium) chopped onion
- 200g (7oz) spinach, washed and chopped

FOR SERVING

- 30g (1oz) melted butter

METHOD

1. Sift flour and salt, make a well in the centre and add water.
2. Mix with a large knife until soft dough forms, knead lightly until smooth then rest for 10-15 minutes.
3. Melt butter in frying pan and sauté onions for several minutes.
4. Add spinach and cook over low heat until liquid evaporated and set aside.
5. Take pastry and divide into walnut sized pieces then roll out into circles on a floured board until a couple of millimetres thick.
6. Spread spinach mixture over half of pastry circle, close over and seal by pressing firmly.
7. Heat a non-stick pan until very hot and cook gozleme one at a time, turning once when browned.
8. Spread with butter and stack to keep warm and allow to soften before serving.

"GÖZLEME"
Ayşe Fahriye, Ev Kadını, no. 369.

Notes

1. Pre-prepared yufka may be used and if not available a double layer of filo pastry is a reasonable substitute.
2. Spinach and onion, spicy potato and minced meat are popular alternative fillings.

Meat, Fish and Poultry

Lamb (and mutton) dishes dominate this section as this was the preferred meat in the 19th century and continues to be popular today. Veal or beef can be substituted in any of these recipes. It is important to note in the braised lamb (and mutton) dishes, according to the cooking methods of the 19th century, the first step is to briefly boil the meat. This step is not mentioned in the Priest's Braised Veal (Dana etiden Papaz Yahnisi) recipe. As mentioned in the introduction, this may be related to the belief that meat for Muslims may need to be 'cleaned', with the scum from the broth being removed.

In the original recipes containing meat, the cut and the fat content is mentioned. The meat was generally fatty and from a mature sheep (mutton). These days most people prefer to consume beef or veal.
Fish and fish recipes existed in Istanbul in the 19th century. Before this period the consumption of fish and seafood was relatively scarce in the kitchens of the elite. The fish recipes selected in this section are simple but allow the flavour of the fish to dominate.

As with the red meat dishes, other poultry can be substituted for chicken in the Stuffed Chicken (Tavuk Dolması) recipe as the stuffing is suitable for all fowl.
In the 19th century all meat, fish and poultry were cooked following the same methods. Fish, chicken or lamb were stewed with onions, grilled or roasted.

Kebab with Yoghurt

YOĞURTLU KEBAB

Serves 4

INGREDIENTS

- 600g (1lb 5oz) lamb, chopped into 2.0cm cubes
- juice of 600g (3 large) onion
- 1/4 teaspoon salt
- 1/4 teaspoon freshly cracked black pepper
- 300g (10oz) fresh flat bread, cut in half lengthways if thick
- 200g (7oz) butter
- 150ml (5floz) meat stock
- 500g (1lb2oz) yoghurt
- 4 large cloves garlic, finely chopped

METHOD

1. Marinate lamb in onion juice for several hours.
2. Prepare charcoal in barbeque (or grill).
3. Skewer lamb pieces and place on rack over charcoal.
4. Spread 80g (3oz) butter on bread and lay over lamb as it cooks.
5. Heat stock and keep warm.
6. In a separate pan, melt remaining butter.
7. In a large bowl, mix yoghurt, garlic, salt and pepper together.
8. Remove when lamb browned all over.
9. Cut bread in small squares and lay half in bottom of serving dish
10. Lay meat across bread, and remaining bread around edges.
11. Pour over stock, spoon over yoghurt and butter.
12. Serve.

"YOĞURTLU KEBAP"
Ayşe Fahriye, Ev Kadını, no. 115.

Bird Kebab

KUŞ KEBABI

Serves 4

INGREDIENTS

- 800g (1 3/4 lb) lamb, chopped into 2-3cm cubes
- juice of 600g (3 large) onion
- 1/4 teaspoon salt
- 1/4 teaspoon freshly cracked black pepper
- 1/4 teaspoon cumin
- large pinch cinnamon
- 1 teaspoon flour

METHOD

1. Marinate lamb in onion juice mixed with salt, pepper, cumin and cinnamon for several hours.
2. Prepare charcoal in barbeque (or grill).
3. Skewer lamb pieces and place on rack over charcoal.
4. While browning and juices running sprinkle with flour and continue to rotate over coals until cooked.
5. Serve.

Note *Bird Kebab is a literal translation of Kuş Kebabı. Traditionally, butchers would cut meat for the kebab the size of a bird's head.*

KUSH KEBABİ
Cut as much as is wanted of mutton or lamb in pieces the size of walnuts; then pour a small teacup of raw onion-juice over, mixed with sufficient salt and pepper; rub it well in, and let them remain for about two hours; then pass them on the skewers one by one, place them in front of a moderate fire, and turn them continually. As soon as the meat begins to get brown, and the gravy drops, sprinkle a little flour over. When the meat is thoroughly done, sprinkle a little cinnamon and cumin over, and serve hot.
Türabi Efendi, A Manual of Turkish Cookery, no. 16.

Twice Cooked Lamb Chops

SULU PİRZOLA KIZARTMASI
Serves 4

INGREDIENTS
- 16 thin lamb loin chops, flattened
- 45g (1 1/2 oz) butter
- 2 large (400g) onion, chopped
- 2 large (400g) tomato, deseeded and chopped
- 5-6 stems parsley, chopped
- 1 teaspoon salt
- 1 teaspoon rosemary leaves

METHOD
1. Prepare charcoal in barbeque (or grill).
2. Grill meat over coals until brown.
3. In a large frying pan melt butter, sweat onion and tomato and remove.
4. Place chops in bottom of pan, cover with onion and tomato mixture, sprinkle with parsley, salt and rosemary leaves (and a little water if mixture dry).
5. Cover and cook over very low flame for 45 minutes until soft.
6. Serve.

Note *Charcoal-grilled meat has a distinctive flavour that a conventional grill cannot replicate.*

"SULU PİRZOLA KIZARTMASI"
Mahmud N. Tosun, Aşçı Başı, no. 22.

Braised Lamb and Garlic

SARIMSAKLI YAHNİ

Serves 4

INGREDIENTS
- 150g (1 medium) onion, sliced
- 20g (3/4oz) butter
- 800g (1 3/4 lb) lamb, chopped into 2.0cm cubes
- 30 small- medium cloves, peeled
- 30ml (1floz) grape vinegar
- 1/4 teaspoon pepper
- 1/4 teaspoon cumin
- salt

METHOD
1. Sauté onions in butter until beginning to brown.
2. Lay half lamb in the base of a pan, cover with garlic then remaining lamb.
3. Add onions, vinegar, pepper, cumin and water to just cover.
4. Bring to boil and simmer until tender.
5. Season and serve.

SARIMSAKLİ YAHNİ
"Cut some mutton into pieces the size of walnuts, peel a sufficient quantity of garlic, mix two teaspoonfuls of salt, one of pepper, and one of cumin; then lay seven or eight cloves of garlic on the bottom of a stewpan, sprinkle a pinch of the seasoning, then add some pieces of mutton, and so forth, until the whole is laid; then add two or three slices onions, fried in fresh butter, a teacup and half of a vinegar, and three of water, set it on a charcoal fire, and let it simmer until the meat is nicely browned and tender, dish up, and serve."
Türabi Efendi, A Manual of Turkish Cookery, no. 41.

Lamb with Dried Plums

ERİKLİ YAHNİ
Serves 4

INGREDIENTS
- 600g (1lb5oz) lamb (shoulder), trimmed of excess fat and chopped into 2cm cubes
- 300g (2 medium) onion, grated
- 60g (2oz) butter
- 200g (7oz) dried plums, de-stoned
- 3 teaspoons sugar
- 2 sticks cinnamon
- 1 teaspoon salt

METHOD
1. Place meat in a large pan, just cover with water and bring to the boil.
2. Reduce heat and simmer for a few minutes, removing scum that rises to top.
3. Remove meat and reserve meat stock.
4. Strain onion juice from grated pulp.
5. Place onion juice and meat in a bowl and mix thoroughly then allow to sit for 10 minutes.
6. Heat butter in large pan and brown meat over medium-high heat.
7. Add remainder of juice and onion pulp and continue to cook until onion browns.
8. Add prunes and cook a further 5 minutes.
9. Add meat stock, sugar, salt, cinnamon stick and cook over low heat until meat is tender and juices evaporated (allow 1 hour).
10. Serve.

Note
1. Chestnuts, dried apricots and quince may be used in place of plums.
2. If plums are very dry, soak in hot water for several minutes.

"KESTANE, AYVA VE KURU KAYISI VE KARA ERİKLİ YAHNİLER"
Ayşe Fahriye, Ev Kadını, no. 148.

Braised Veal with Onions

DANA ETİNDEN PAPAZ YAHNİSİ

Serves 4

INGREDIENTS

- 800g (1 3/4 lb) lean veal, chopped and washed
- 400g (14oz) small pearl onions, peeled
- 8 large cloves garlic, peeled and chopped
- 1 teaspoon salt
- 1/2 teaspoon freshly cracked black pepper
- 1 teaspoon cumin
- 60ml (2 floz) good quality grape vinegar

FOR SEAL

- 150g (5 1/2 oz)flour
- 125ml (4floz) water

METHOD

1. Preheat oven to 180oC/350oF/gm4.
2. Place veal and onions in earthenware casserole dish sprinkle over remaining ingredients and over with lid.
3. Mix flour and water to a smooth dough and seal casserole dish.
4. Cook in oven for approximately 1 hour.
5. Serve.

Note *Red wine may be used in place of vinegar.*

DANA ETİNDEN PAPAS YAHNİSSİ
"Cut five or six pounds of a loin of veal in pieces the size of eggs, place them in rather deep earthen stewpan, with three or four sliced onions, five or six heads of garlic, salt and pepper, a little cumin, and a teacup of wine vinegar, without water; put the cover over the pan air tight, or paste it round with paper, so that no steam shall escape; put it in an oven, or simmer it on a moderate fire for about three or four hours. When done, dish it up tastefully, and serve. Be particular in pasting round the cover, and the fire must not be fierce, or the meat may burn."
Türabi Efendi, A Manual of Turkish Cookery, no. 38.

Kofte with cumin

KİMYONLU KÖFTE

Serves 4

INGREDIENTS
- 600g (1lb5oz) minced lamb
- 300g (2 medium) grated onion
- 2 cloves garlic, minced
- 1 egg, beaten
- 2 teaspoons cumin
- 1 teaspoon salt
- 1 teaspoon freshly cracked black pepper
- seasoned flour for coating
- vegetable oil or clarified butter for frying

METHOD
1. Place meat, onion and garlic in large bowl and combine.
2. Add egg, cumin, salt and pepper and mix well.
3. Shape into small, flattened circles and lightly coat with flour.
4. Heat a small amount of oil in a frying pan until almost smoking.
5. Cook a few köfte at a time, allowing pan to re-heat after each batch.
6. Keep warm and serve.

Note
1. Kofte can be cooked under a grill. In this case omit the egg in the mixture and do not coat in flour before cooking.
2. Serve with sliced onions and chopped parsley.

GHİMYONLU KYUFTE
"Mince very fine as much as is wanted of either raw mutton or beef, with two or three onions peeled; sprinkle sufficient salt, pepper and cumin; then knead well and make it up in the shape of small buns, and fry them in fresh butter, or broil them on a gridiron a nice brown. When done, arrange them in a dish, and serve hot, with chopped parsley mixed with thinly slices onions round the dish."
Türabi Efendi, A Manual of Turkish Cookery, no. 62.

Stuffed Chicken

TAVUK DOLMASI

Serves 4

INGREDIENTS

- 1.75g (1 large) whole chicken
- 20g (3/4 oz) butter
- 100g (1 small) onion, finely chopped
- 30g (1oz) chicken liver, cleaned and chopped
- 15g (1/2 oz) pine nuts
- 15g (1/2 oz) currants
- 100g (3 1/2 oz) rice, washed
- 1/4 teaspoon salt
- 1/4 teaspoon freshly cracked black pepper
- 1/4 teaspoon ground cinnamon

FOR GLAZE

- juice from 50g (1/2 small) grated onion
- 1 egg yolk, beaten

METHOD

1. Wash chicken and remove any stray feathers.
2. Preheat oven to 200oC/400oF/gm6.
3. Melt butter in a small pan, add onion, chicken liver, pine nuts and sauté for a few minutes.
4. Add currants, rice, pine nuts, salt, pepper and cinnamon, mix well then add water to just cover, place lid on tightly and cook over medium heat until rice just beginning to become tender and water absorbed.
5. Place chicken in a large oven tray, stuff with pilaf, rub onion juice into skin then paint with egg yolk.
6. Bake for 35 minutes or until juices clear.
7. Remove and rest for 15 minutes before carving and serving.

Note *Turkey, duck or pheasant may be used in place of chicken.*

PİLİC DOLMASSİ

"Get two or three chickens, well clean them, sprinkle a little salt over, and let them for ten minutes or so; then chop up the livers, hearts and the gizzards, very fine, place them in a frying pan with sufficient butter; then add three-quarters of a pound of well-washed rice, two or three tablespoonfuls of pistachios, a table spoonful of currants, sufficient salt and pepper, and a little cinnamon, stir round for a few minutes; then add a small teacup of hot water, and keep stirring till the water is absorbed and the rice partly soft; then stuff the chickens with it; sew them up; and fry them a nice brown in fresh butter; then place them in a stewpan, nearly cover them with broth put the pan on a charcoal fire with the cover over, and let them simmer till the chickens are quite tender. Dish up, and serve."

Türabi Efendi, A Manual of Turkish Cookery, no. 114.

Griddled Chicken

TAVUK KÜLBASTISI

Serves 4

INGREDIENTS

- 500g (2 1/2 large) onion
- 1.5kg (1 medium) chicken
- 1/2 teaspoon freshly cracked black pepper
- 20g (3/4 oz) butter

METHOD

1. Grate onions and press pulp over a sieve to extract juice.
2. Cut chicken into 6 pieces, remove obvious bones, flatten with a mallet and remove skin.
3. Place chicken pieces, onion juice and pepper in a bowl and marinate for a minimum of 2 hours in refrigerator.
4. Preheat a griddle pan, grease with butter and cook chicken a few pieces at a time basting with marinade then brush with butter when cooked.
5. Serve.

"TAVUK KÜLBASTISI"
Ayşe Fahriye, Ev Kadını, no. 117.

Red Mullet Baked in Paper

KAĞIT İÇİNDE TEKİR BALIĞI

Serves 4

INGREDIENTS

- 4 sheets baking parchment
- 16 small red mullet, washed
- salt
- freshly cracked black pepper
- 3-4 handfuls parsley leaves
- 30ml (1floz) olive oil
- 30ml (1floz) vinegar
- 30ml (1floz) water
- olive oil for greasing paper

METHOD

1. Pre-heat oven to 180oC/350oC/gm4.
2. Spread baking parchment on a baking tray and grease with olive oil.
3. Lay four fish side-by-side on half of the paper.
4. Sprinkle with salt, pepper, 1/4 parsley and 1teaspoon each olive oil, vinegar and water.
5. Fold paper over and seal by rolling and crimping the edges to make an envelope.
6. Repeat for each serving.
7. Place tray in oven and bake for 12 minutes.
8. Remove and place sealed envelopes on individual plates.
9. Serve immediately.

"KAĞIT İÇİNDE TEKİR BALIĞI"
Yeni Yemek Kitabı, p. 15.

Monkfish and Bay Leaf Kebabs

DEFNELİ FENER BALIĞI KEBABI

Serves 4

INGREDIENTS

- 800g (1 3/4 lb) monkfish, cubed
- 300g (2 medium) onion, chopped
- 1 teaspoon salt
- bay leaves
- olive oil
- parsley
- lemon

METHOD

1. Wash fish, dry and place in a large bowl with onion and salt, leaving to marinate for 1 hour.
2. Take fish and skewer between bay leaves then brush with olive oil.
3. Heat griddle to very hot temperature and cook kebabs for several minutes on each side.
4. Serve garnished with parsley and lemon.

Note *Bonito, swordfish or mackerel can be used in place of monkfish*

"DEFNELİ KILIÇ VE PALAMUT KEBABI"
Mahmud N. Tosun, Aşçı Başı, no. 51.

Vegetables with Meat

Some of the recipes in this section are familiar while others are less so. Most surprisingly is the absence of tomato in all but one dish and the frequent use of cinnamon as a condiment. In all the recipes, meat is used as a flavouring if not a key ingredient. The type of meat used can be pieces or minced, lamb or beef, or omitted all together in dishes such as Okra (Bamya) or Summer Vegetables Braised with Lamb (Yaz Türlüsü). The stuffed dishes, Stuffed Globe Artichoke (Enginar Et Dolması) and Vine Leaves Stuffed with Meat (Adi Yaprak Dolması) can also be made with a meat-free stuffing (see Rice Stuffed Vine Leaves with Sour Cherries (Vişneli Yalancı Yaprak Dolması) for rice-based stuffing). Interestingly the name changes to 'liars' for 'false' (yalancı) dolma as meat is no longer included in the recipe!

Summer Vegetables Braised With Lamb

YAZ TÜRLÜSÜ

Serves 6

INGREDIENTS

- 200g (7oz) medium fat lamb, chopped
- 100g (1 small) onion, sliced
- 300g (3 small, long) eggplant, peeled in stripes and chopped
- 300g (2 large) tomatoes, chopped
- 300g (2 large) zucchini or gourd, scraped and sliced
- 110g (4oz) green beans, ends and sides trimmed
- 75g (15-20) okra, tops trimmed
- 60ml (2 floz) tomato juice
- 2 teaspoons salt
- 1 teaspoon pepper
- 40g (1 1/2 oz) butter

FOR DOUGH TO SEAL CASSEROLE DISH

- 150g (5 1/2 oz)flour
- 125ml (4floz) water

METHOD

1. Place meat in a large casserole dish then vegetables in layers, with those requiring least cooking time on top.
2. Sprinkle with tomato juice, salt, pepper, butter and cover with lid.
3. Mix flour and water to a very soft dough and press around seal of casserole dish.
4. Cook over a low heat for 45 minutes or until liquid released from vegetables is absorbed.
5. Serve hot.

Not

1. *When preparing okra, care must be taken not to trim too much to prevent the stew from becoming sticky.*
2. *This casserole can be cooked in a medium oven.*
3. *A range of other vegetables can be used in this dish.*

"YAZ TÜRLÜSÜ"
Ayşe Fahriye, Ev Kadını, no. 212.

Baked Eggplant

PATLICAN MÜCMERİ

Serves 4

INGREDIENTS

- 900g (4 large long) eggplant
- 30g (1 oz) butter
- 300g (2 medium) chopped onion
- 250g (9oz) minced lamb
- 1/2 bunch parsley, chopped
- 1 teaspoon salt
- 1 teaspoon pepper
- 2 eggs, beaten
- olive oil
- 1 lemon, halved

METHOD

1. Preheat oven to 180°C/350°F/gm4.
2. Cut eggplant lengthways making sure to leave one edge intact, scoop out the inside leaving a small amount of flesh under the skin then rub with lemon to prevent discolouration.
3. Drop eggplant flesh into boiling water, simmer for 5 minutes then drain.
4. Heat a frying pan, melt butter and brown onions, add meat, parsley, salt, pepper, boiled eggplant flesh and continue to cook until meat browned then remove from heat.
5. Add eggs and stir.
6. Place eggplant on a tray greased with olive oil, stuff base of each with meat mixture then close lid.
7. Bake for 25 minutes or until eggplant soft.
8. Serve.

Note *Traditional mücmer (mücver) contain minced meat, eggs and herbs and is fried.*

BADİNJAN MUJMERİ
"Procure six or seven egg plants, cut them in two lengthways, take out the insides, and boil them a little in water, moderately salt; then take them out, and put them in a basin, add three or four finely chopped onions, previously fried a nice brown in fresh butter, four or five tablespoonfuls of fried minced meat (prepared of raw mutton), a handful of parsley, chopped fine, sufficient salt and pepper, and two or three eggs well beaten up, and mix them well together; then butter a baking-pan, in which arrange half of the egg-plants, and stuff them with the above mixture; cover them with the remaining half, and bake them in a rather hot oven. When the egg-plants are shrunk and soft, they are cooked. Dish up, and serve."
Türabi Efendi, A Manual of Turkish Cookery, no. 68

‘Shaken’ Eggplant

PATLICAN SİLKMESİ

Serves 4

INGREDIENTS

- 500g (5 small, long) eggplant, peeled in stripes and sliced in 1-1.5cm pieces
- 15g (1/2 oz) butter
- 250g (9oz) medium fat lamb, diced in 2cm pieces
- 150g (1 medium) onion, chopped
- 300ml (1/2 pint) water
- 30ml (1floz) tomato juice
- 1/2 teaspoon salt
- 1/4 teaspoon freshly cracked black pepper
- salt for soaking eggplant
- vegetable oil for frying eggplant

METHOD

1. Place eggplant in a large bowl, sprinkle liberally with salt, cover with water and set aside for several minutes, drain and pat dry.
2. Melt butter in large pan and brown meat over high heat then remove.
3. Brown onion in same pan then add meat, 200ml (7floz) water, cover and cook until tender (about 1 hour).
4. Meanwhile heat vegetable oil in a medium flat-based pan.
5. When a cube bread browns within 5-6 seconds, fry eggplant, several pieces at a time, ensuring oil returns to appropriate temperature between batches.
6. Drain on paper towel.
7. When meat is tender, add eggplant, tomato juice, salt, pepper and remaining water, cover and cook a further 5-6 minutes.
8. Serve.

Note *Salting eggplants draws out moisture (and any bitterness) and concentrates flavour.*

ADİ SİLKME
“Cut three or four pounds of mutton into small pieces as above, wash and dry them in a cloth, then place them in a stewpan with sufficient salt and pepper, set it on the fire, and stir with a wooden spoon until it begins to hiss, which indicates that all the moisture is dispersed; then add three or four ounces of fresh butter, and keep stirring till the meat is nicely browned. When done, take them out with a hand-strainer, and place them in a dish; keep it hot; then cut three or four egg-plants in thin slices, sprinkle them with salt, and let them remain for a few minutes. When the bitter juice is drawn down from them, fry them a nice colour on both sides in the remaining fat from the meat, then arrange them tastefully over the meat, or round the dish, sprinkle a little pepper over and serve hot.”
Türabi Efendi, A Manual Of Turkish Cookery, No. 101 .

Okra

BAMYA

Serves 6

INGREDIENTS

- 200g (7oz) lean lamb, chopped into small pieces
- 1 teaspoon salt
- 30g (1oz) butter
- 150g (1 medium) onion, chopped
- 500g (90-100) okra, tops trimmed
- 2 teaspoons pomegranate syrup or verjuice
- 1/2 teaspoon pepper
- 1/2 teaspoon cinnamon

METHOD

1. Place meat in a large pan, just cover with water and bring to the boil and add salt.
2. Reduce heat and simmer for a few minutes, removing scum that rises to top.
3. Remove meat and reserve meat stock.
4. Sauté onion in butter, mix with meat and lay on bottom of large pan.
5. Wash okra, strain and place on top of meat, add pomegranate syrup then cover with reserved meat stock.
6. Cover and bring to boil then simmer until okra tender.
7. Serve warm with sprinkling of pepper and cinnamon.

Note
1. When preparing okra do not trim too much as dish will become sticky.
2. Okra is washed just prior to adding to pan to reduce the stickiness of the final dish.

BAMYA BASTISSI

"Cut three or four pounds of mutton into pieces about the size of walnuts wash and place them in a saucepan with sufficient salt cover them with water and set the pan on the fire. When boiling skim and simmer until the meat is half done then fry partly brown five or six sliced onions in fresh butter then peel the stalky parts and cut off the ends of one or two hundreds okras then place the pieces of meat and the okras together with the onions in layers as above add the liquor in which the meat was boiled if not enough add some of broth and a little salt put the cover over the pan and set it on a charcoal fire until the meat and the okras are tender and a nice gravy is formed at the bottom which you will perceive by holding the pan on one side. Just five minutes before removing it from the fire add the juice of one or two lemons and when done dish up sprinkle a little pepper and cinnamon over and serve."

Türabi Efendi, A Manual of Turkish Cookery, no. 93.

Hünkâr's Kebab

PATLICAN HÜNKÂRBEĞENDİ

Serves 4

INGREDIENTS

FOR TAS KEBAB

- 800g (1 3/4lb) medium fat lamb, chopped in 2cm cubes
- 450g (3 medium) onion, chopped
- 1 1/2 teaspoon salt
- 3/4 teaspoon freshly cracked black pepper

FOR EGGPLANT PUREE

- 1.8kg (6 large) round eggplant
- salt
- pepper

METHOD

1. Preheat oven to 180°C/350°F/gm4.
2. Mix lamb, onion, salt and pepper thoroughly, kneading by hand, then leave to marinate for a 2-3 hours.
3. Place in small glass ovenproof dish and upturn into a large pan.
4. Cook over a low heat until juices evaporated.
5. Meanwhile pierce eggplants and place in oven until skin darkens.
6. Remove, allow to cool, peel and puree.
7. Season with salt and pepper to taste and spread in serving dish with lamb in middle.
8. Serve.

Note *The eggplant puree in modern Hünkâr Beğendi Kebab's will contain a béchamel sauce and sometimes kaşar (firm, yellow) cheese providing a creamier, richer base for the meat.*

"BADINCAN HÜNKÂRBEĞENDİ"
Yeni Yemek Kitabı, p. 7.

Vine Leaves Stuffed with Meat

YAPRAK DOLMASI

Serves 4

INGREDIENTS

- 200g (7oz) fresh grape vine leaves
- juice of one lemon
- 200g (7oz) medium fat minced lamb
- 100g (1 small) chopped onion
- 85g (3oz) cracked rice, washed
- 3 tablespoons chopped parsley
- 1/2 teaspoon salt
- 1/2 teaspoon freshly cracked black pepper
- 30ml (1floz) water
- 30g (1oz) butter

METHOD

1. Bring a large pan of water with lemon juice to boil.
2. Place vine leaves in water and simmer for 2 minutes, remove, refresh in cold water and set aside.
3. Place lamb, onion, rice, parsley, salt, pepper and water in a bowl and knead until thoroughly combined.
4. Lay large and broken vine leaves on the bottom of a large pan.
5. Take remaining vine leaves one at a time, trim stem and place a teaspoon full of filling across the base of leaf.
6. Fold bottom and sides of leaf across filling and roll tightly.
7. Put in pan, seam side down, lining dolma around the edges of the pan first, packing firmly together.
8. Lay any remaining leaves on top, cover with water and place a small plate over the dolma to keep in place and bring to boil.
9. Reduce heat, simmer for 30 minutes, add butter and continue to cook until leaves are tender.
10. Allow to cool and serve.

Notes

1. *Serve with yoghurt.*
2. *Hazelnut, quince, mallow or spinach leaves may be used in place of grape vine leaves.*
3. *Preserved grape leaves can be used however they need to be soaked thoroughly to remove salty brine.*
4. *For a meatless alternative, use the stuffing from 'Rice stuffed vine leaves with sour cherries' and omit sour cherries.*

ADİ YAPRAK DOLMASSI

"Prepare some vine leaves as No. 111; then chop up fine a sufficient quantity of raw mutton with one or two onions, add three or four tablespoons of rice well washed, a little salt and pepper, and mix them well together with a little water, to make it like a paste; the lay the vine leaves open, put in each one a teaspoonful of this stuffing; and wrap them up about the length and the thickness of your thumb; squeeze them gently with your hand one by one, that they may retain the stuffing while cooking; then place them in a saucepan without any water, and set it on the fire with the cover over. When their own moisture is exhausted, add some broth and let it simmer until it forms a nice gravy at the bottom; then take one out and try if the meat and the rice are done; if not, add some broth. When the rice and the meat are quite tender, dish up and serve."

Türabi Efendi, A Manual of Turkish Cookery, no. 115.

Stuffed Artichoke

ENGİNAR ET DOLMASI

Serves 4

INGREDIENTS

- 4 medium artichokes
- 2 lemons, halved
- 200g (7oz) minced lamb
- 100g (3 1/2 oz) cracked rice, washed
- 150g (1 medium) chopped onion
- 7-8 stems each parsley, dill and mint, chopped
- 1/2 teaspoon cinnamon
- 1 teaspoon salt
- 1 teaspoon freshly cracked pepper
- 30ml (1 floz) water
- 60g (2oz) butter

METHOD

1. Prepare artichoke by removing stem, pulling off outer leaves and cutting off top third and rubbing flesh with lemon.
2. Boil in salted water for 5 minutes and refresh in cold water.
3. Scrape out hairy choke and rinse thoroughly.
4. Place meat, rice, onion, herbs, cinnamon, salt, pepper and water in a bowl and knead until thoroughly mixed.
5. Stuff each artichoke, leaving one centimetre at the top.
6. Place in large pan, half fill with water, add butter and bring to the boil.
7. Cover, turn down heat and simmer for 45 minutes or until leaves tender, rice cooked and liquid reduced to an oily consistency.
8. Gently remove artichokes and serve with remaining reduced liquid.

"ENGİNAR ET DOLMASI"
Ayşe Fahriye, Ev Kadını, no. 279.

Braised Dried Beans with Pastırma

FASULYE YAHNİSİ

Serves 4

INGREDIENTS

- 350g (12oz) dried white beans, soaked overnight
- 40g (1 1/2 oz) butter
- 200g (1 large) onion, chopped
- 60g (2oz) pastırma (without fenugreek), soaked in water
- 1 teaspoon red pepper flakes
- 1 teaspoon salt
- 400ml (14floz) water

METHOD

1. Place beans in a large pan, cover well with water, bring to boil then simmer until beans start to become tender.
2. Melt butter and saute onions.
3. Add pastırma , red pepper, salt and continue to brown for several minutes.
4. Add beans, water and bring to the boil, then simmer until beans tender and liquid reduced to oily consistency.
5. Serve.

Notes

1. Pastrami can be used in place of pastırma, however will not need to be soaked.
2. For a vegetarian dish, omit pastırma.

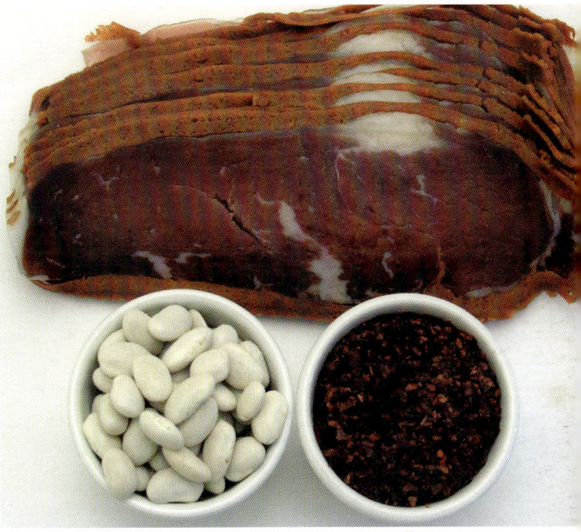

"FASULYA YAHNİSİ"
Ayşe Fahriye, Ev Kadını, no. 144.

Pilavs

Pilav is a staple accompaniment to many dishes in today's Turkish cuisine. In 19th century Ottoman cuisine it was served alone as a main dish to end the feast. The arrival of pilav and hoşaf signaled the end of festivities. The recipes for rice pilavs include a Classic Pilav (Adi Pilavi) and Sultan Hünkâr Pilav (Hünkâr Pilavı) rich in meat and nuts and fit for a king. The Oven Baked Pasta (Fırın Makaronya) may seem surprising but familiar with its macaroni, cheese, egg and tomato but reflects European influence in the cuisine of the elite during the latter years of the 19th century.

Classic Pilav

ADİ PİLAV

Serves 4

INGREDIENTS

- 400g (14oz) pilav rice
- 800ml (1 pint 8oz) water or veal stock
- 1 1/2 teaspoons salt
- 60g (2oz) butter

METHOD

1. Rinse rice thoroughly for several minutes under running water.
2. Place in large pan, add water or stock and salt, stir, cover and bring to the boil, reduce heat and cook until the liquid has been absorbed (approx. 20 minutes).
3. Remove the pan from the heat, add butter and stir, cover with a clean cloth, press the lid down firmly and allow to steam for about 15 minutes.
4. Serve.

Note *Small holes appear in the surface of the cooked rice when all the water has been absorbed.*

ÂDİ PİLAV
"Pour two pints of water in saucepan and put it on the fire. When boiling throw in a pound of best rice well washed and sufficient salt and boil it until the whole of the liquid is absorbed then put in a saucepan half of a fresh butter and set it on the fire until it boils then pour it all at once over the rice put the cover over the pan wrap a wet cloth round it to prevent the steam for escaping and keep it on the hop for half and hour then take the lid off and stir it once round with a fork you will find that each grain is swollen and is well separated then dish up in the shape of a dome and serve hot."
Türabi Efendi, A Manual of Turkish Cookery, no.121.

Eggplant Pilav

PATLICANLI PİLAV

Serves 4-6

INGREDIENTS

- 400g (2 medium-large) eggplant, peeled in stripes and chopped
- 150g (1 medium) chopped onion
- 60g (2oz) butter
- 500ml (17floz) boiling water
- 1 teaspoon salt
- 1 teaspoon freshly cracked black pepper
- 1/4 teaspoon crushed mastic
- 1 large pinch saffron
- 400g (14oz) pilav rice, washed

METHOD

1. Boil eggplant in salted water for 5 minutes, strain and set aside.
2. Melt butter in large frying pan and saute onions over medium heat.
3. Add eggplant and cook a further few minutes.
4. Add water, salt, pepper, mastic, saffron and allow to come to the boil.
5. Add rice, stir and cover.
6. Cook over very low heat for 20-25 minutes or until rice fluffy.
7. Remove from heat, place a clean cloth over the rice and replace lid, allow to stand for 10-15 minutes.
8. Serve.

Note *Eggplant can be fried in oil for a richer flavour.*

BADİCANLI PİLAW
"Procure three or four egg-plants, cut them in four crossways, take out the inside, if seeded, and cut them in slices about an inch thick; then scald them in salt water, and drain them; then put three-quarters of a pound of fresh butter in a saucepan with one or two chopped onions; put it on fire, and let the onions stew. When nearly brown, add the pieces of eggplants, and fry them partly together with the onions; then add two pints of hot or cold water, and one of broth, a little salt, and pepper, a few pieces of gum-mastic, and a small quantity of saffron. As soon as it boils, add a pound and half of rice, well-cleaned, and let it boil slowly until the liquor is absorbed; then take it off, and place it on the hob for ten minutes or so. Dish it up, serve."
Türabi Efendi, A Manual of Turkish Cookery, no.129

Hünkâr's Pilav

HÜNKÂR PİLAVI

Serves 4-6

INGREDIENTS

- 400g (14oz) rice
- 60g (2oz) butter
- 500g (1lb2oz) lamb, chopped into 1.5-2.0cm cubes
- 600ml (1 pint) water or reserved meat stock
- 60g (2oz) pistachios, toasted
- 30g (1oz) currants
- 3/4 teaspoon mixed spice
- 1 1/2 teaspoons salt

METHOD

1. Wash and soak rice for 15 minutes then strain.
2. At the same time place lamb in a large pan, add water to cover and 1/2 teaspoon salt, bring to the boil removing scum as it rises to top, remove from heat then strain and reserve stock.
3. Melt butter in large frying pan and quickly brown meat over medium-high heat.
4. Add rice, cook for a few minutes then add water or stock, pistachios, currants, mixed spice, salt then stir and cover.
5. Bring to boil then reduce heat and simmer for 20 minutes or until rice tender.
6. Remove from heat, place a clean cloth over rice and replace lid and allow to stand for 10-15 minutes.
7. Serve.

KHUNKYAR PİLAWİ
"Wash two pounds of the best rice put it in a clean cloth, tie it and hang it up; then cut two pounds and a half of the choice part of mutton in pieces about the size of walnuts, wash and place them in a stewpan with four pints of water and put it on a charcoal fire. When boiling skim it well add sufficient salt and let it simmer for twenty or thirty minutes; then drain the liquor into a basin, put half a pound of fresh butter over the pieces of meat and fry them a nice brown; then add three pints of the liquor with a little salt, three or four tablespoonfuls of pistachios, the same of minced raw mutton, previously fried a nice color in fresh butter, one or two of currants, and half of teaspoonful of mixed spice. As soon as it boils, add the rice and boil it for two or three minutes longer; then reduce the heat of the fire by removing burning coals; and leaving only the ashes and the sparks, put on the pan with the cover over for about an hour; the dish up tastefully, and serve." Türabi Efendi, A Manual of Turkish Cookery, no.131.

Oven Baked Pasta

FIRIN MAKARONYA

Serves 4-6

INGREDIENTS

- 300g (10 1/2 oz) macaroni (no3)
- 1 egg, beaten
- 150g (5oz) cheese, grated
- 400g (2 large) tomatoes, peeled, deseeded and chopped finely
- 1 tablespoon flour
- 1/2 teaspoon salt
- 1/2 teaspoon freshly cracked black pepper
- 30g (1oz) butter, chopped in small pieces

METHOD

1. Preheat oven to 180°C/350°F/gm4.
2. Boil macaroni in salted water, drain and run under cold water to separate.
3. Mix egg, cheese, tomatoes, flour, salt and pepper together.
4. Lay macaroni in a tray and cover with cheese and tomato mixture.
5. Sprinkle with butter, place in oven and bake until golden brown (12-15 minutes).
6. Serve hot.

"FIRIN MAKARONYA"
Yeni Yemek Kitabı, p. 16.

Desserts

The Ottomans had a passion for sweet things and this desire was reflected in the range of sugary, rich desserts that were created. Fruit, milk, pastry, sugar and nuts dominate the dessert recipes in this section. Some familiar and expected while others surprising and re-discovered. Coiled Baklava (Sarığıburma) and Turkish Delight with Rosewater (Ratahül Hulkum) may be known but Honey, Rosewater and Musk Helva (Güllabiye Helvası) is an exotic sweetmeat from the past.

The Turkish cream, 'kaymak', is thick and rich enough to be rolled and sliced. Some references cite 'clotted cream', a well-known product from Devon or Cornwall in England as a substitute. If you cannot buy kaymak, making a substitute from milk and thickened cream will produce a good result (see Cooking Techniques and Tips).

Jams in Ottoman cuisine were eaten by the spoonful as a sweet treat. They are generally quite liquid with pieces of fruit or flowers suspended throughout and perhaps resemble fruits preserved in thick sugar syrup.

Coiled Baklava

SARIĞIBURMA

Serves 8

INGREDIENTS

FOR DOUGH

- 500g (1lb 2oz) white flour
- 2 eggs, beaten
- 15g (1/2 oz) butter, melted
- 10ml (1/3 floz) olive oil
- 200ml (7floz) water with 1/2 teaspoon salt dissolved

FOR ROLLING

- 200g (7oz) starch

FOR BRUSHING DOUGH

- 250g (9oz) butter, melted and cooled

FOR FILLING

- 300g (10 1/2 oz) walnuts, chopped
- 30g (1oz) icing sugar
- 45ml (1 1/2 floz) water

FOR SYRUP

- 800g (1 3/4 lb) sugar
- 400ml (14floz) water
- 1 teaspoon lemon salt

METHOD

1. Sift flour onto work surface and make a large hole in the centre.
2. Place eggs, butter and olive oil in middle and mix in a circular motion, drawing in flour from outside.
3. When sticky add water and continue to mix until a soft dough is formed.
4. Knead well until very smooth and elastic then allow to rest for 15 minutes under a clean cloth.
5. Knead and rest a further three times.
6. Meanwhile, place walnuts in a food processor and pulse until finely ground.
7. Remove, add sugar and water and mix well.
8. Roll dough out to 30cm (12in) log shape and cut into ten even sized pieces.
9. Shape each piece into a ball then allow to rest a further 15 minutes.
10. Liberally dust working surface with starch and roll out each piece of dough to 20cm circle then allow to rest again for 10 minutes.
11. Beginning with the first pastry sheet, continue to roll each out until almost transparent and 30-40cm in diameter.
12. Pre-heat oven to 200°C/400°F/gm6.
13. Brush one sheet with butter, place a second sheet over the top then sprinkle one half with walnut mixture.
14. Roll up with thin rolling pin (1.5cm (1/2 in) diameter.
15. Crinkle pastry roll by pushing toward the middle from each end.
16. Push off rolling pin and cut into three.
17. Lay in 40cm (15in) tray, placing as if making a large coil.
18. Pour remaining melted butter over the pastry.
19. Bake until brown on top and base golden, leave to cool on wire rack.
20. Make syrup by gently dissolving sugar and lemon salt in water.
21. Pour hot syrup over cool pastry and allow to soak for several hours, turning occasionally.
22. Serve.

Note *Pre-prepared baklava yufka may be used and if not available filo pastry is a good substitute.*

"SARIĞIBURMA"
Ayşe Fahriye, Ev Kadını, no. 427.

Shredded Pastry with 'Kaymak' and Syrup

KAYMAKLI KADAYIF

Serves 8

INGREDIENTS

- 250g (9oz) fresh shredded pastry
- 90g (3oz) butter
- 500g (1lb2oz) sugar
- 250ml (9floz) water
- 1/4 teaspoon lemon salt
- 200g (7oz) kaymak
- 120g (4oz) walnuts, chopped

METHOD

1. Divide pastry and place in bases of two 25cm round trays, ensuring that pastry is uniformly and tightly packed.
2. Melt butter and while hot, brush liberally over pastry.
3. Place over a low heat and gently brown the pastry on both sides.
4. Add sugar, water and lemon salt in a pan and bring boil then allow to cool slightly.
5. Lay cream over one pastry base, sprinkle with three-quarters of walnuts then place second over top.
6. Pour syrup over ensuring all pastry is covered.
7. Allow pastry so soften, sprinkle with walnuts, cut and serve.

KAYMAKLİ KADAYİF
"Prepare four pounds of vermicelli, as No. 149; lay half of it in a buttered tin, pour in each about half a pound of scalded fresh butter, and bake them a delicate colour on both sides. When cooked, strain and wash out all the butter from both, as above; then lay some clotted cream over one, half an inch thick, and cover it with the other one; then pour hot syrup all over, as n.149, and put it again in the oven until the syrup is nearly absorbed; then cut it in any shape you fancy, or turn it on to a dish it is, and serve."
Türabi Efendi, A Manual of Turkish Cookery, no. 152.

Honey, Rosewater and Musk Helva

GÜLLABİYE HELVASI

Serves 6

INGREDIENTS

- 300g (10 1/2 oz) honey
- 100g (3 1/2 oz) butter
- 250g (9oz) wheat starch
- 450ml (16floz) water
- 60g (2oz) toasted, slivered almonds
- 1 teaspoon rosewater
- 1/8 teaspoon musk, ground and mixed with rosewater

METHOD

1. Place honey in large flat based pan, gently heat then add butter, stir and take off the heat.
2. Mix starch with enough water to form a smooth but runny batter then add remainder of water.
3. Slowly add starch slurry to honey, stirring continuously and when well incorporated add almonds and rosewater with musk then return to heat.
4. Continue to stir over low-medium heat until mixture thickens to a very stiff paste and starch cooked.
5. Spread in a flat-based tray, allow to cool, cut into diamond-shaped pieces and serve.

Note *To make a smooth batter when mixing starch with water, make a small well in the centre and slowly add cold water, stirring to draw flour into the middle.*

GHYULABİYE
"Put a pound of loaf sugar in a stew-pan, with a pint of water, and set it on the fire: when boiling, add half a pound of fresh butter, a pound of wheat-starch, previously formed into a thin batter with water, a quarter of a pound of skinned almonds, and three or four tablespoonfuls of rose-water, mixed with a little musk, and stir it gently until it becomes crummy; then spread it in a rather deep dish, press it all over with the back of the spoon, cut it up in diamonds, and serve with a little sugar sifted over."
Türabi Efendi, A Manual of Turkish Cookery, no. 171.

Semolina Helva with Milk and Almonds

İRMİK HELVASI

Serves 4-6

INGREDIENTS

- 250g (9oz) semolina
- 250g (9oz) sugar
- 100g (3½ oz) butter
- 450ml (16floz) milk
- 55g (2oz) almonds

METHOD

1. Melt butter in large frying pan, add semolina and almonds and toast over a low heat, stirring constantly (approximately 20 minutes).
2. Place milk and sugar in a separate pan and bring to the boil, ensuring all sugar has dissolved.
3. Carefully add milk syrup to semolina and stir thoroughly.
4. Cover and continue to cook over medium heat for 5 minutes then turn heat off and leave for 10 minutes.
5. Serve warm.

IRIMİK HELWASSİ
"Set on the fire a stewpan, with a three-quarters of a pound of fresh butter; when hot, add gradually a pound and six ounces of sago, with four ounces of skinned almonds, and keep stirring it until the almonds are a nice brown; then pour in all at once a pint and a half of boiling milk, with boiling syrup, which you have previously made of a pound and a half of loaf sugar and a pint and a half of water; stir it well, put the cover over, and let it remain for fifteen minutes; then sprinkle a little-rose-water over, dish up, shake some sugar over, and serve."
Türabi Efendi, A Manual of Turkish Cookery, no. 173.

Classic Milk Pudding with Vanilla

VANİLYALI MUHALLEBİ

Serves 4-6

INGREDIENTS

- 1 litre (1 3/4 pints) full-fat milk
- 100g (3 1/2 oz) rice flour
- 60g (2oz) granulated sugar
- 2 teaspoons vanilla essence

METHOD

1. Place milk in a large pan, bring to boiling point then remove from heat.
2. Meanwhile, mix rice flour with enough water to form a smooth but runny batter.
3. Pour rice slurry into milk, stirring continuously then add sugar and vanilla and continue to stir.
4. Return to the heat and slowly bring to the boil over a medium heat while stirring then simmer for 3-4 minutes until thickened.
5. Pour into serving dishes and chill until firm.
6. Serve.

Note *To make a smooth batter when mixing rice flour with water, make a small well in the centre and slowly add cold water, stirring to draw the flour into the middle.*

"VANİLYALI MUHALLEBİ"
Ayşe Fahriye, Ev Kadını, no. 462-63.

Almond, Hazelnut, Pistachio and Pinenut Pudding

KEŞKÜL-İ FUKARA

Serves 6

INGREDIENTS

- 85g (3oz) almonds, skinned and roughly chopped
- 85g (3oz) hazelnuts, skinned and roughly chopped
- 85g (3oz) pistachios, skinned and roughly chopped
- 85g (3oz) pine nuts, skinned and roughly chopped
- 950ml (1 pint 13floz) full cream milk
- 140g (5oz) granulated sugar
- 40g (1 1/2 oz) wheat starch

METHOD

1. Place nuts in a food processor and process until finely ground then set aside 40g for garnish.
2. Bring 900ml milk up to boil in a large pan, reduce heat, add sugar and dissolve then remove from heat.
3. Stir remaining milk into starch until a smooth batter is formed.
4. Slowly add starch slurry to milk while stirring continuously then add nuts.
5. Return to a low heat and stir until thickened.
6. Pour into serving dishes, cool then refrigerate.
7. Serve with remainder of nuts sprinkled over top.

Note
To make a smooth batter when mixing starch with water, make a small well in the centre and slowly add cold water, stirring to draw the flour into the middle.

"KEŞKÜL-İ FUKARA"
Ayşe Fahriye, Ev Kadını, no. 486.

Lemon Jelly

LİMON ELMASİYESİ

Serves 6

INGREDIENTS

- 250g (9oz) sugar
- 1litre (3/4 pints) water
- 9 gelatine leaves
- 150ml (5floz) lemon juice
- rind of one lemon

METHOD

1. Place sugar in a pan and dissolve in 300ml water, bring to boil, reduce until syrup becomes oily then remove from heat.
2. Meanwhile place gelatine in a dish and cover with cold water.
3. Add lemon juice and rind to syrup and briefly bring to boil.
4. Remove from heat again, add gelatine leaves, stir until dissolved then make up to 1 litre with remaining water.
5. Pour into dishes and refrigerate until set.
6. Serve garnished with cream and crystallised lemon rind.

Notes

1. *Other fruits containing juice can be used.*
2. *3 gelatine leaves = 12g powdered gelatine and will set 600ml / 1 pint liquid unless liquid contains acid such as lemon juice. If making jelly with other less acidic fruits use 5-6 leaves in the above recipe. More gelatine will be needed if the jelly is to be turned out of mould.*

LİMON ELMASSİYYESSİ
"Dissolve about an ounce of isinglass in a small tumbler of water, boil and reduce it to half, then pass it through a cloth into a basin; then cut in two five lemons, take off the rind of one of them and remove the pith, place them in a basin, and squeeze the juice of the lemons into it; then put half a pound of loaf sugar in a stewpan with a pint of water, set it to boil until it becomes a syrup, then take it off and add the juice and the rind of the lemons, put the stewpan again on the fire with the cover over. As soon as it begins to boil, skim it well, and add three wine -glasses of water by degrees, which will assist its clarification; let it boil one or two minutes longer, then add the isinglass, pass it through a jelly-bag, if fancied, add two tablespoonfuls of rose water, and then pour it into a mould and place it on ice. When ready, dip the mould in warm water and turn it out. If summer, add a little more isinglass."
Türabi Efendi, A Manual of Turkish Cookery, no. 180.

Stuffed Dried Plums and Dates

ERİK VE HURMA DOLMASI

Makes 18 pieces

INGREDIENTS

- 50g (6 large) dried yellow plums
- 50g (6 large) dried black plums
- 150g (6 large) dried dates
- 120g (4oz) sugar
- 150ml (5floz) water
- 60g (2oz) almond, slivered and lightly toasted

METHOD

1. Place dried fruit in a pan, cover with water and gently simmer until fruit tender and beginning to become soft.
2. Remove, reserving liquor and peel away any excess skin from fruit and remove stones.
3. Dissolve sugar in water and bring to the boil, simmer for a few minutes until syrup thickens slightly then allow to cool slightly.
4. Stuff fruit with almonds and place on serving tray.
5. Pour syrup over fruit and serve.

Note *Serve with home made kaymak (see Cooking Techniques and Tips).*

"TERKİB-İ ERİK TOLMASI"
Et-Terkibat Fi Tabhi'l-Hulviyyat, p.11.

Egg Crepes with Sweet Apricot Puree

KAYISI EZMELİ KAYGANA

Serves 4

INGREDIENTS

FOR APRICOT PUREE

- 200g (7oz) sugar
- 100ml (3 1/2 floz) water
- 2 pinches lemon salt
- 250g (9oz) apricots, peeled, halved and de-stoned

FOR CREPES

- 5 medium eggs
- 50g (1 3/4 oz) wheat starch

METHODS

1. Dissolve sugar in water in a large pan, add lemon salt and bring briefly to boil.
2. Add apricots and simmer until soft, then remove apricots and reserve syrup.
3. Puree apricots and set aside.
4. Beat eggs until fluffy.
5. Make a paste with starch and a little egg mixture.
6. Add paste to eggs, stirring to a smooth batter.
7. Heat a small (non-stick) frying pan and pour in 1/6 batter.
8. Cook for several minutes on each side until golden brown then repeat until mixture used.
9. Take one crepe, spoon on 1/5 apricot puree and repeat four times, then finish by placing last crepe on top.
10. Pour over warmed syrup, cut in four then serve.

Note

1. A lighter crepe can be made by replacing 2 eggs with 100-120ml milk.
2. Serve with cream.

"KAYISI EZMELİ KAYGANA"
Ayşe Fahriye, Ev Kadını, no. 450.

"KAYMAKLI KAYGANA"
Ayşe Fahriye, Ev Kadını, no. 448.

Turkish Delight with Rosewater

RAHATÜ'L-HULKUM

Makes 50 pieces

INGREDIENTS

FOR TURKISH DELIGHT

- 450g (1lb) sugar
- 750ml (1 pint 6floz) water
- 75g (2 1/2 oz) wheat starch
- 20ml (2/3floz) rosewater

FOR GREASING TRAY (20cm x 20cm)

- almond oil

FOR COATING

- 110g (4oz) icing sugar
- 110g (4oz) wheat starch

METHOD

1. Dissolve sugar in water, bring to boil then reduce to simmer.
2. Mix starch with enough water to form a smooth but runny slurry.
3. Remove syrup from heat and gradually add starch slurry, stirring continuously.
4. Add rosewater, return to heat and cook over gentle heat until mixture very thick.
5. Test by dropping a small amount onto icing sugar, when the mixture no longer absorbs any sugar it is done.
6. Meanwhile grease tray with almond oil and pour in mixture.
7. Allow to cool, cut and drop into icing sugar / starch mixture, coat then dust off excess and serve.

Note *Turkish Delight can be stored in an airtight container for 6 months.*

RAHATİ-L-HOLKUM

"Put in a very clean stewpan two pounds and three quarters of loaf sugar, with four quarts of water, and stir with a wooden spoon until the sugar is dissolved; then set it on a moderate charcoal fire, and immediately add eight ounces and half of fine wheat starch by degrees, stirring it at the same time so as to prevent it from getting lumpy, and continue stirring it from the bottom of the pan until it forms a smooth substance; then take a little out, and let drop a few drops on powdered sugar. If it moistens or absorbs the sugar it is not done, and if it does not it is done. Then mix a little musk, the size of small pea, in a less than a quarter of a pint of rosewater, and add this to it; stir it for half a minute or a minute longer; then take it off and pour it into a convenient dish or a plated pan about an inch deep, which you have previously oiled with almond oil. When cold, cut it in pieces an inch broad and two long, and dip them in sifted sugar mixed with half the quantity of fine wheat starch. See that they are well covered, to prevent them from sticking to each other, and serve as a dessert. This celebrated and delicious confection may be kept for a long time in a wooden box, such as a fig-box."

Türabi Efendi, A Manual of Turkish Cookery, no. 192.

Rose Jam

GÜL REÇELİ

Makes approximately 3kg

INGREDIENTS
- 100g (3 1/2 oz) pink or red edible rose petals
- 2.5kg (5 1/2 lb) sugar
- 800ml (1pint 8floz) water
- 3 teaspoons lemon salt

METHOD
1. Trim the white part from bottom of rose petals and set aside.
2. Lay half of the rose petals in the bottom of a glass or ceramic dish, cover with 75g sugar then remaining rose petals and another 75g sugar.
3. Cover and leave in refrigerator overnight.
4. Meanwhile add whites of petals to water and bring to boil over a medium heat, simmer for 10 minutes then allow to cool and refrigerate.
5. Take rose petal mixture and knead to a paste then return refrigerator for a further night.
6. Place rose petal paste in a large pan, add remainder of sugar and water and bring to a boil then simmer for 30 minutes.
7. Add lemon salt, stir and simmer a further 5 minutes, check that jam will set by placing a spoonful in the refrigerator for a few minutes (the jam should set to a runny consistency).
8. Pour into previously prepared containers and seal.

GHYULBE-SHEKER
"When the roses are in full bloom, gather about a pound of the leaves, pick out the large ones, and cut the white ends off with a pair of scissors; then put the small ones and the white ends in a very clean stewpan with three-quarters of a pint of water, and scald them; then pass the liquor through a piece of muslin or a sieve, squeeze well the leaves and throw them away; then put the liquor in the pan with three pounds and half of white sifted sugar, and stir them with a wooden spoon till the sugar is dissolved; then add the large leaves that you have picked out, stir and boil till rather thick; or try a little on a plate; if it sets then remove it from the fire. When cold, fill the preserve jars, cover them air-tight and keep them in a rather cool place."
Türabi Efendi, A Manual of Turkish Cookery, no. 253.

Fruit Compotes, Cordials and Sherbets

Fruit Compotes (Hoşaflar) have a particular method that sets them apart from other fruit drink preparations. Pieces of fruit are set aside before the drink is prepared and added before serving. The remainder of the fruit is boiled with sugar unless the fruit is fragile, such as mulberries, where it is simply mixed with sugar and water then pushed through a sieve. Hoşaflar are traditionally served with a spoon and eaten like a soup.

Cordials (Şuruplar) are a confection of fruit and sugar, boiled to a thick consistency, pushed through a sieve and served diluted with water and ice.

Sherbets on the other hand are fruit kneaded with sugar, left to develop flavour and colour then mixed to taste with water and ice. The recipe Lemonade with Mint (Naneli Limonata) is one example.

Lemonade with Mint

NANELİ LİMONATA

Makes 1 litre

INGREDIENTS

- zest of 1 1/2 lemons
- 100g (3 1/2 oz) sugar
- 25-30 mint leaves, extra for garnish
- 150ml (5floz) lemon juice
- 800ml (1 pint 8floz) water

METHOD

1. Mix lemon zest, sugar and mint leaves in a bowl, kneading thoroughly by hand.
2. Allow to sit for 1-2 hours to develop colour and flavour.
3. Add lemon juice and water, stir and serve strained over ice with mint garnish.

Note *Other soft fruits may be used in place of lemon.*

"LİMONATA"
Ayşe Fahriye, Ev Kadını, no. 630.

Black Mulberry Juice

KARADUT HOŞAFI

Serves 6

INGREDIENTS
- 500g (18oz) black mulberries
- 200g (7oz) sugar
- 650ml (1 pint 2floz) water
- 1 teaspoon orange blossom water

METHOD
1. Trim the stems from half mulberries and set aside.
2. Mix remaining mulberries with sugar and push through sieve.
3. Add orange blossom water and whole mulberries.
4. Pour over ice and serve.

Note *Other soft fruits may be used in place of mulberries.*

"BÖĞÜRTLEN HOŞAFI"
Melceü't-Tabbahin, p. 77.

Peach Cordial

ŞEFTALİ ŞURUBU

Makes 500-600ml (1pint)

INGREDIENTS
- 800g (1 3/4 lb) sugar
- 400ml (14floz) water
- 600g (21oz) peaches, peeled and de-stoned
- 15ml (1/2floz) lemon juice

METHOD
1. Dissolve sugar in water in a large pan and bring briefly to boil.
2. Add peaches and simmer until resembles jam.
3. Pass through a sieve 2-3 times then return to cleaned pan.
4. Bring to boil, reduce heat, add lemon juice, stir then cool.
5. Mix 75ml (2 1/2 floz) cordial with 500ml (17floz) water (or according to taste) and add ice to serve.

"TAZE KAYISI ŞURUBU"
Ayşe Fahriye, Ev Kadını, no. 543.

Glossary

Albanian cheese	Arnavut peyniri	Fresh white cheese
Dessert, a type of	Aşure	Kind of Ottoman -Turkish pudding made of boiled grains and seasoned with nuts and dried fruits.
Baklava	Baklava	A range of sweet dishes popular in Ottoman – Turkish cuisine made with layers of paper-thin pastry, generally filled with ground nuts and soaked in sugar syrup.
Fish gelatin	Balık tutkalı	A kind of gelatin extracted from fish that was used in making fruit jelly 'elmasiye' in 19th century Ottoman cuisine.
Okras	Bamya	A popular vegetable in Ottoman-Turkish cuisine since 17th century.
Vegetable stew generic name for a kind of	Bastı	Slowly cooked vegetables with small pieces of meat and a little water.
Cheese, white	Beyaz peynir	A soft to hard cheese made mostly from cow's milk and matured in brine in Ottoman – Turkish cuisine. Feta cheese is a suitable alternative.
Pastry / pie	Börek	Generic name of Ottoman – Turkish pastries. Mostly savoury pastries or pies with various fillings. Numerous varieties exist from small fried pastries to large lasagne-style pies.
Floral water	Çiçek suyu	Essences of flowers such as orange blossom used to flavour sweet dishes and beverages used in Ottoman cuisine.
Mackerel, salted and dried	Çiroz	Mackerel, salted and dried A popular type of meze in 19th century Ottoman cuisine.
Soup	Çorba	
Nigella seeds	Çörek otu	Small, black aromatic seeds about the same size as sesame seeds, sometimes mistakenly called 'black cumin'.
Dirhem		Unit of weight in Ottoman kitchens 1 Dirhem = 3.148g
Stuffed / Filled	Dolma	Generic name of stuffed dish, often vegetable but also fowl, mussels or meat in Ottoman – Turkish cuisine.
Jelly	Elmasiye	Fruit-based gelatine dessert made in Ottoman cuisine.
Bread, flat-style	Fodula	A diminuative of pide.
Savoury filo-style pancake	Gözleme	A flat 'pancake' style made with yufka and stuffed with cheese, herbs, minced meat found in Ottoman–Turkish cuisine.
Rosewater	Gül suyu	Essence of rose petals used to flavour sweet dishes and beverages in Ottoman cuisine.
Rose Dessert	Güllaç	Ottoman and Turkish dessert made from thin filo pastry made of starch, soaked in syrup and flavoured with rosewater.
Caviar	Havyar	Black and red caviar consumed largely in Istanbul during the 19th century.
Helva	Helva	Generic name for a range of sweetmeats made from a variety of ingredients. The nougat-style helva with sesame seeds, sugar and nuts as well as one based on flour or starch were popular from the Ottoman period until today.

Compote	Hoşaf	Generic name of fruit drink made with whole fruit pieces, fruit juice and sugar syrup in Ottoman - Turkish cuisine.
Sultan	Hünkâr	
Zucchini	Kabak	Courgette
Dessert, type of	Kadayıf	Three main desserts are named kadayıf. Sweetened shredded pastry (tel kadayıf), a type of cake soaked in syrup (ekmek kadayıfı), and small flat dough circles fried in butter and soaked in syrup (yassı kadayıf) in Ottoman - Turkish cuisine.
Cheese, yellow Cheddar-style	Kaşar peynir	A medium to firm cheese eaten fresh (taze) or matured (eski) where it resembles a peccorino or grana padano. Popular both in Ottoman and Turkish cuisine.
Crepe	Kaygana	Kind of crepe made with eggs and served with kaymak and syrup in Ottoman cuisine.
Cream (Clotted)	Kaymak	Rich thick cream that can be rolled and sliced. Made by gently simmering water buffalo milk until a thick 'skin' forms. Contains 60% fat. Consumed in both Ottoman and Turkish cuisine.
Kebab	Kebap	Generic name of any kind of griddled or roasted meat in Ottoman cuisine.
Cumin	Kimyon	Found as small dark yellow seeds or ground powder, the best flavour is obtained by grinding seeds just before using.
Kıyye		Unit of weight in Ottoman kitchens 1 Kıyye = 400 Dirhem
Kofte (Meatballs)	Köfte	Any dish where the ingredients are minced or pounded then formed into small flattened balls and fried or grilled. Traditionally and today kofte is made generally from minced meat.
Verjuice	Koruk	Unripe grape juice.
Griddle	Külbastı	A form of kebab where meat is first griddled on a hot plate or griddled and briefly braised in a small amount of liquid in Ottoman cuisine.
Water of ashes	Küllü su	The clear portion of a mixture of water and ashes used in Ottoman pastry making to make dough crispy.
Lamb	Kuzu	Any meat taken from an animal that is less than 1 year old.
Bonito, in brine	Lakerda	Bonito preserved in brine. Traditional Ottoman meze in 19th century Istanbul.
Lemon Salt	Limon Tuzu	Crystals of lemon acid used in making jams. Sustitute with lemon juice.
Dessert, kind of	Lokma	Ottoman and Turkish dessert made of batter fried in oil and soaked in syrup.
Turkish Delight	Lokum	Traditional Ottoman dessert made with starch and syrup flavoured with nuts, rose water masti or fruit juices.
Pasta	Makaronya	'Makarna' in today's Turkish cuisine.
Ravioli, Turkish	Mantı	Ravioli-style pasta filled with minced meat served with yogurt yoghurt in Ottoman - Turkish cuisine.
Musk	Misk	Extracted from the glands of a musk deer and found as grains or powder. The scent is both penetrating and lingering and tiny amounts are used in cooking in Ottoman cuisine.
Fried dish, generic name for a type of	Mücmer (or mücver)	Kind of pancake made of minced meat, eggs and sometimes of vegetables fried in butter or in olive oil in Ottoman cuisine.
Pudding, generic name of	Muhallebi	Generic name of pudding in Ottoman - Turkish Cuisine.

Vegetable stew, generic kind of	Musakka	Generic name for a kind of vegetable stew make with name of minced meat in Ottoman – Turkish cuisine.
Pomegranate syrup	Nar ekşisi	A thickness juice made from pomegranate seeds, often with a tangy flavour used especially in South-Eastern Turkish cuisine.
Rose, type of	Okka gülü	A kind of edible rose used in making jams and syrups in 19th century Istanbul.
Stew, kind of	Papaz yahnisi	Fish or veal stew prepared by Christian population of Istanbul in the Ottoman empire. Literally means stew of priest.
Pastrami, a spicy, dried type	Pastırma	Cured, dried fillet of beef coated in a paste of fenugreek, cumin and red pepper that has been known to Turkish cuisine since the Ottoman period. Cut into thin slices, it is eaten alone or as an ingredient in savoury dishes.
Eggplant	Patlıcan	Aubergine.
Molasses of fruit	Pekmez	A thick syrup made from boiling the juice of fruit especially grape. Used as a sweetener in Ottoman cuisine.
Sweet	Pelte/Paluze	Type of Ottoman sweet made with starch, sugar and fruit juices.
Flat bread / pizza	Pide	A yeast leavened flat bread, made especially during Ramadan and popular in both Ottoman and Turkish cuisine. Pide is eaten with meze and main dishes and used to mop up any excess gravy or juices. Pide is also prepared a little like a boat-shaped pizza with toppings such as kaşar cheese, minced meat or egg.
Olive oil dish, generic name for a type of	Pilaki	Fish, mussels or vegetables cooked in olive oil in Ottoman-Turkish cuisine.
Pilaf (Pilav)	Pilav	Fluffy rice dishes eaten plain or with additional ingredients as a main meal in the Ottoman period and as an accompaniment to main meals in Turkey today.
Turkish Delight	Rahatü'l- hulkum	Ottoman name of Turkish delight. Called 'lokum' in today's Turkish cuisine. Traditional Ottoman dessert made with starch and syrup flavoured with nuts, rose water, mastic or fruit juices.
Rakı	Rakı	Ottoman and Turkish aniseed flavoured drink.
Dessert, kind of	Revani	Ottoman and Turkish dessert made from a baked cake soaked in syrup.
Saffron	Safran	The stigma of the crocus flower it is used to both flavour and colour sweet and savoury dishes. The most potent and expensive is grown in Iran and Spain. Turkish saffron is a lower quality and used in larger quantities. Saffron was a popular condiment in Ottoman cuisine.
Mastic	Sakız	Resin from the acacia tree, it is used to make the chewy ice-cream famous in Turkey. Chewing gum is also known as 'sakız'. Mastic is used to flavour puddings and also found in savoury dishes from the Ottoman period.
Salad	Salata	Generic name of salad made with vegetables, herbs or seafood in Ottoman-Turkish cuisine.
Sahlep	Salep	Powder made from orchid roots. Beverage of hot milk, sugar and sahlep powder.
Baklava, a kind of	Sarığıburma	A coiled baklava made by rolling several sheets of filled pastry on a rolling pin, crinkling, cutting and placing many similar pastries in a tray as if coiled. It is likely that this was named after the coiling of a turban worn on the head in Ottoman times.
Vermicelli	Şehriye	Thin noodles often used in soups.
Sherbet	Şerbet	A non-alcoholic drink made from fresh fruit or spices mixed with

		sugar and water in Ottoman cuisine.
Vegetable stew, generic	Silkme	Vegetables such as eggplant or zurrchini fried in butter,name for a kind of added to pre-cooked pieces of mutton then simmered.
Bread ring	Simit	A sesame coated bread ring made from heavy dough that is poached in pekmez and then baked. Known since Ottoman times.
Syrup	Şurup	Sugar and water mixed in a 2:1 ratio then boiled briefly before being used in numerous desserts and drinks in Ottoman – Turkish cuisine. Cordials are also known as şurup and are a syrup confection of fruit and sugar.
Sesame seeds	Susam	Cream coloured, small, oily seeds used as a topping on breads, the base of tahini and in commercially produced helva.
Rice pudding	Sütlaç	Type of Ottoman and Turkish pudding made of rice and milk
Sauce, nut and garlic purslane	Tarator	Sauce made from walnuts, hazelnuts, almonds or pine nuts, garlic, bread and lemon juice and served with fish, mussels, calamari, or spinach. Known in 19th century Ottoman cuisine.
Cinnamon	Tarçın	A popular spice in 19th century ottoman cuisine.
Frying pan / fried	Tava	Fried dishes or the pan used to cook them.
Blanc mange	Tavuk göğsü	Type of Ottoman medieval pudding made of chicken breast, milk and sugar or honey.
Shrimp	Teke	Small prawns found in the Marmara Sea.
Liasion	Terbiye	Classic thickener of Ottoman - Turkish cuisine. Made from egg yolks and lemon and added to dishes as a flavouring or thickener.
Butter	Tere yağı	Most butter sold in Turkey is low in salt and high in milk solids as it was in the Ottoman period. Using clarified butter was the normal practice in Ottoman kitchens.
Cheese ripened	Tulum peyniri in sheepskin	Strong flavoured cheese originally matured in sheepskin. Today it is aged in skins or synthetic bags.
Ratatouille, type of	Türlü	Stew of mixed vegetable seasoned with small pieces of meat in Ottoman – Turkish cuisine.
Pickle	Turşu	Fruit or vegetable based meze, prepared and preserved in vinegar or brine that has been known in Turkish cuisine since the Ottoman period.
Stew	Yahni	Made with meat, onions and often other vegetables or fruits in Ottoman – Turkish cuisine.
Yoghurt	Yoğurt	Popular accompaniment to many savoury dishes.
Filo-type pastry	Yufka	Thin sheets of pastry, rolled to varying thickness according to the dish. Used in making some börek, baklava and gözleme in Ottoman – Turkish cuisine.
Pudding, type of	Zerde	Type of Ottoman pudding made with rice, water and saffron.
Olive Oil	Zeytinyağı	Used throughout current day Turkish cooking but known in its own right when braised with vegetables and eaten cold as 'zeytinyağılı' or 'with olive oil'.
Sweat		To soften onions slowly in butter or oil, often with a lid firmly placed over pan.

Bibliography

OTTOMAN COOKBOOKS

"A Manual of Turkish Cookery" in *İlk Basılı Türkçe Yemek Kitabı Melceü't-Tabbâhîn*, (First Published Ottoman Cook Book –Refuge of Cooks) ed. Kut, Cüneyt, Unipro: İstanbul, 1997.

Ayşe Fahriye, *Ev Kadını (House Wife)*, İstanbul: Mahmud Bey Press, 1882-1883

Et-Terkibat Fi Tabhi'l- Hulviyyat (Tatlı Pişirme Tarifleri),(Recipes of desserts) ed. Kut, Günay., Ankara: Turkish Culture and Tourism Ministry, 1986.

İlk Basılı Türkçe Yemek Kitabı Melceü't-Tabbâhîn (Aşçıların Sığınağı),(First Published Ottoman Cook Book Refuge of Cooks) ed. Kut, Cüneyt, Unipro: Istanbul, 1997.

Mahmud Nedim BinTosun, *Aşçı Başı, (The Chef)* Istanbul: Kasbar Library, 1900.

Mehmet Kamil, *Melceü't-Tabbâhîn,(Refuge of Cooks)*, Istanbul: 1844

Türabi Efendi, *A Manual of Turkish Cookery*, London:1864.

Yeni Yemek Kitabı, (New Cook Book), Istanbul:1882-1883.

GENERAL BIBLIOGRAPHY

Arsel, Semahat (ed), *Timeless Tastes Turkish Culinary Culture*, Istanbul: Mas Matbaası, 1996.

Artan Tülay, "Aspects of the Ottoman Elite's Food Consumption: Looking for "Staples," "Luxuries" and "Delicacies" in a Changing Century" in *Consumption Studies and the History of the Ottoman Empire 1550-1922* , ed. Quataert, Donald, State University of New York Press, 2000, p. 107- 200.

Balıkhane Nazırı Ali Rıza Bey, *Eski Zamanlarda Istanbul Hayatı*,(Life in Istanbul in Old Days) ed. Çoruk, Ali Şükrü. Istanbul: Kitabevi., 2001.

Bilgin, Arif, *Osmanlı Saray Mutfağı, (Ottoman Palace Cuisine)*, Istanbul: Kitabevi, 2004.

Castellan, Antoine Laurent. *Illustrations de l'Histoire des Othomans*, Paris: Nepheu, 1812

Ertürk, Necip, *Türk Tatlı Sanatı, (Turkish Art of Patisserie)*, Istanbul: Remzi , 2003.

Fenn-i Tabahat. İstanbul: 1340 (1920-21).

Halıcı, Nevin, *Türk Mutfağı, (Turkish Cuisine)*, Ankara: Güven, 1990.

Işın, Mary Priscilla, *Mahmud Nedim bin Tosun Aşçıbaşı, (Mahmud Nedim bin Tosun The Chef)*, YKY: Istanbul, 1998.

Leith, P. & Waldegrave, *C. Leith's Cookery Bible* (2nd edition), Bloomsbury Publishing Plc, London, 1996

Kut, Cüneyt (ed),*İlk Basılı Türkçe Yemek Kitabı Melceü't-Tabbâhîn (Aşçıların Sığınağı)*,(First Published Ottoman Cookbook Refuge of Cooks), Unipro: Istanbul, 1997.

Kut, Turgut, *A Bibliography of Turkish Cookery Books up to 1927*, London: Petit Propos Culinaire, PPC 36, 1990.

Mantran, Robert, *17. Yüzyılın İkinci Yarısında İstanbul, (Istanbul during the second half of 17th century)* Ankara: TTK, 1990.

Oberling. G. Smith, Grace Martin, *The Food Culture of the Ottoman Palace*, İstanbul: Mas Press.

Osmanlı Dünyası, 37. Müzayede, de Péra Müzayede Evi, 2001.

Osmanlı Dünyası, 46. Müzayede, de Péra Müzayede Evi, 2003.

Osmanlı Dünyası, 53. Müzayede, de Péra Müzayede Evi, 2003.

Osmanlı Dünyası, 60. Müzayede, de Péra Müzayede Evi, 2003.

Reindl-Kiel, Hedda. "The Chickens of Paradise Official meals in the mid-seventeenth century Ottoman Palace" in *The Illuminated Table*, the Prosperous House, ed. Faroqhi.S., Neumann, Germany: Ergon in Kommission, 2003, p.89-127.

Samancı, Özge. "Culinary Consumption Patterns of the Ottoman elite during the first half of the nineteenth century" in *Illuminated Table the Prosperous House*, ed. Faroqhi, S. Neumann, Germany: Ergon in Kommission, 2003, p. 161-185.

Samancı, Özge. "19. Yüzyıl İstanbul Mutfağında Yeni Lezzetler",(New tastes in Istanbul's Cuisine during the 19th Century) *Yemek ve Kültür,(Food & Culture)* Istanbul: Çiya Publications, 2006, no. 4, p. 86-98.

Samancı, Özge, *Continuity and Change in the Culinary Culture of the Ottoman Palace in 19th Century* , Unpublished MA thesis, Istanbul: Boğaziçi University Social Sciences Institute, 1998.

Yerasimos, Marianna, *500 Years of Ottoman Cuisine*, İstanbul: Boyut Publishing Group, 2005.

Yerasimos, Stéphane, *A la Table Du Grand Turc (Sultan's Table)*, Paris : Sindbad Actes Sud, 2001.

A Brief Guide to Turkish Pronunciation

The Turkish Language is phonetic, so in some ways an easy language to sound out. With few exceptions all letters are pronounced with very similar stress.
The Turkish alphabet has the following 29 letters;
Aa, Bb, Cc, Çç, Dd, Ee, Ff, Gg, Ğğ, Hh, İi, Iı, Jj, Kk, Ll, Mm, Nn, Oo, Öö, Pp, Rr, Ss, Şş, Tt, Uu, Üü, Vv, Yy, Zz

There are eight vowels:
Aa as a in apple;
Ee as e in egg;
İi as i in tin;
Iı as er pronounced in butter (butt-uh!);
Oo as o in pot;
Öö as ir in dirt;
Uu as u in put;
Üü as ew in few.

The consonant sounds that differ significantly to English are:
Cc, as in j in jade;
Çç as ch in check;
Gg as g in get;
Ğğ is a silent or soft sound and prolongs the sound of the preceding letter as in sağ (sa-a);
Jj as in s in treasure;
Şş as sh in shape;
Vv as w in weave, quite a soft w;
Rr and Hh are both sounded out even is at the end of a word;

When consonants are together both are sounded as in teşekkürler (tesh-ek-kur-ler) or thanks!

Standard Measures

ENGLISH	TURKISH	su bardağı water glass*	çorba kaşığı tablespoon	teaspoon/tatlı kaşığı
		g	**g**	
bulgar	bulgur	200	12	
flour	un	120	9	3
semolina	irmik	160	10	
dried beans	kuru fasulye	160		
pasta (macaroni)	makarna	160		
pasta (rice)		100		
corn flour	mısır unu	150	9	
lentils	mercimek	160	12	
chickpeas	nohut	160	12	
wheat starch	nişasta	120	9	
rice	pirinc	200	12	
icing sugar	pudra şekeri	120	12	
granulated sugar	toz şeker	200	15	5
salt	tuz		20	5
yoghurt	yoğurt	210		
currants	kuş üzümü		15	
sultanas/ raisins	üzüm		15	
almond	badem	100	6	
margarine	margarin		15	5
butter	tereyağı		15	5
		ml	**ml**	ml
water	su	200	15	5
milk	süt	200	15	5
olive oil	zeytinyağı	200	15	5
vegetable oil	sıvı yağ	200	15	5

* the 'water glass' is a standard 200ml measurement used in household kitchen in Turkey

1 tablespoon
Australian measure 20ml
European / United States measure 15ml

1 cup
Australian / European / United States 250ml

Measurements- Solids

oz	lb	G	oz	lb	g
0.25		8	13		370
0.50		15	14		400
0.75		20	15		425
1		30	16	1	450
1.5		40	18		505(500)
2		55	29	1.25	560
3		85	24	1.5	675
3.5		100	28	1.75	790(800)
4	0.25	110	32	2	900
5		140	lb	kg	
6		170		2.2	1.0
7		200		3	1.35
8	0.5	225		4	1.8
9		255(250)		5	2.3
10		285		6	2.7
10.5		300		7	3.2
11		310		8	3.6
12	0.75	340		9	4.0
				10	4.5

Measurements-Liquids

floz	ml	Other
0.5	15	1 tablespoon
1	30	
2	60	0.25 su bardağı
3	90	
4	120	
5	150	0.25 pint
6	175	
7	200	1 su bardağı
8	230	
9	260(250)	1 cup
10	290	0.5 pint
12	350	
14	405	2 su bardağı
16	460	0.75 pint
18	520	
20	580	1 pint
1000	1.75	pint
1160	2	pints
1450	2.5	pints
1740	3	pints

Oven Temperatures

oC	oF	Gas Mark
70	150	0.25
80	175	0.25
100	200	0.5
110	225	0.5
130	250	1
140	275	1
150	300	2
170	325	3
180	350	4
190	375	5
200	400	6
220	425	7
230	450	8
240	475	8
250	500	9
270	525	9
290	550	9

Index